THE AUTOBIOGRAPHY OF
FIONA PITT-KETHLEY

Volume One: My Schooling

Tamworth Press

First published in 2000
by Tamworth Press
© Fiona Pitt-Kethley 2000

A catalogue record for this book is available from the British Library.

ISBN 0 9509441 4 9

Cover photograph © Graham Tovey

Tamworth Press

Printed in Great Britain by Redwood Books Ltd.

Contents

For my mother, Olive Banfield, 12th August 1915 to May 21st 1999

Chapter One: A Difficult Birth

I WAS BORN at tea time – 17.03 precisely – on 21st November 1954 at Edgware Hospital. My birth was an exceptionally difficult one. I sometimes feel that it set a kind of blueprint for my life. Nothing has come to me easily. When it comes, it's so delayed that half its pleasure has gone. My mother took four days producing me. She probably could have spent a week at it if the doctor hadn't speeded matters towards the end and dragged me out with the aid of the forceps.

Two days or so into her labour she was seen by the specialist. He complained that she was screaming. The ward maid was kinder. "Never mind," she said. "Rome wasn't built in a day." The specialist was also there again at the actual birth and complained again. "I'm in an awful mess!'" my mother remembered him saying. I'd like to think I up and chucked my afterbirth at the bastard.

The first moment my mother realised I was born and alive was when she heard someone screaming much more loudly and much higher than her or any other baby or mother in the hospital. I came into the world doing a top C. In her half-conscious state she also remembers hearing, "It's a girl". She hallucinated a whole long line of women down the centuries repeating these words.

My name was registered as Helen Fiona Pitt-Kethley. My mother wanted Fiona as my first name but thought the combination of names was more mellifluous the other way round. She noticed that it scanned as two dactyls and a trochee.

I am not convinced that anyone actually remembers their own birth in the sensual sense of recalling sights, smells and sounds vividly, but most of us know the facts. I feel I have also retained a certain all round sense of the occasion.

In my earliest years, I was possessed by the need to play a game that involved escaping with difficulty from a dark space. I would crouch in what I now recognise as a foetal position beneath the blankets and coverlets. My mother had to tuck them in under the mattress and attempt to block my exit and make the game difficult. Of course, I always managed to escape into the air after a few attempts. I usually emerged coughing and sneezing from the dusty blankets. I always wanted to play this game in my parents' bed not my own. When I emerged I sometimes said: "Here I am all covered in mud!" My mother never quite worked out how or why I men-

tioned mud. Perhaps I half-recollected someone describing me as
being "covered in blood" in the hospital. By the time I was eight or
so I gave up the game.

After my birth, I was taken away from my mother – both of us
needed rest, they thought. I was left, unwiped and unwashed and
covered in blood. At some stage I was left unattended and, a few
hours later, it was discovered that I'd torn at my face where the
blood had dried and gouged eleven claw marks with my nails on my
left cheek near the chin. I still have the scars. Fortunately they are
colourless so hardly noticeable. If my parents had been rich
Americans I suppose they'd have sued Edgware hospital. As it was,
a nurse put some gentian violet on my wounds and bandaged my
hands until they looked like white lumpy boxing gloves so that I
couldn't get at myself to do any more damage. My father saw me at
this stage. Fortunately he was the type of man who thinks his own
kid is like Helen of Troy even if she's purple with rage and covered
with blood. His only regret was that another baby in the hospital
was even heavier than I was. I weighed in at a hefty nine pounds four
ounces, but one of the boys beat me to being the top weight of the
week by an ounce or two.

Back home, in the next few months, I did become an extremely
beautiful baby – fair and elfin – with short feathery hair on a perfectly formed large skull. I found a tiny snap of my self the other day
and assumed it was someone else. How dare my mother nurse this
fairy child, I thought. What I didn't recognise was my blondness. By
the age of six it had entirely gone. I often think my mother, a former blonde herself held this against me. Even forty years later, she
often said: "When I used to wash your hair it was blonde. I washed
it every day. Perhaps that had something to do with it." She used to
round this statement off with the sort of stare that says: "You filthy
pig. How could you let yourself go like that?"

I was born with the knack of rolling my eyes flirtatiously and
fluttering long eyelashes at any dark men who appeared near my
bed. All the doctors and medical students got the treatment. "Look
at this one. She amuses me," one of the nurses muttered but stopped
the minute she realised my mother was listening intently.

I was a good baby. I cried very little and said and did all the right
things early enough for my parents to be able to boast about me. I
jumped straight from lying down to standing and walking. I've
never been keen on crawling. My legs were prematurely strong due

to the fact that I'd spent most of the time cycling in the air and working out Jane Fonda style while I was supposed to be lying on my back. I'd interrupt the incessant aerobic display only to lift my bottom to have a filled nappy taken away and the new one slid under me. It was rather a convenient trick for my parents. All babies should learn it.

For the first eighteen months of my life my parents lived in a small Edwardian house in Harrow. My father had been brought up in Amersham and worked as a journalist off the Strand. Harrow was a halfway compromise. My mother had done most of the painting needed on the house before they moved in. They were married three years before they had me. They had kept putting a child off to go on holiday. Suddenly my mother realised it was something she shouldn't put off forever. She was thirty-nine when I was born. My father was forty-seven. They were both late-starters.

My father's mother died about a month after they were married. Ellen Pitt-Kethley, née Reed, was a deeply possessive woman. She refused to come to the wedding. Her other son, Andrew, never married. My grandfather, Victor, didn't come to the wedding either, but was friendlier. He died a few months after I was born. I've always felt sorry I didn't get to know him. He was an interesting and witty man, although he could also be mean and selfish. He edited a true travel story magazine called The Wide World for fifty years. His contract required that he only write for George Newnes, so he secretly published a series of ripping yarns under other names – Rupert Chesterton, Singleton Carew, Sidney York, and The Captain. My father was christened after two of these – Rupert Singleton. I have a few of the books. I believe there were many more. The style is atrocious and the substance of the stories naïve. The heroes shout "Caramba!" on every possible occasion. They'd probably have shouted it when they came if he'd written another kind of book. Perhaps he did, under some other name I've never tracked down. His boys' books often had singularly unlikely plots. One of the stories even concerns the smuggling of saccharine. My grandfather never travelled, but thought he had. I found an article by him entitled, "Motoring in Scotland". He couldn't drive and had never been further north than Yorkshire.

My grandfather was also a snob. My surname is a place name in Scotland – a tiny village in Perthshire. My ancestors came from there many generations back and trickled south via Edinburgh. I have my grandfather's birth and marriage certificates. At birth he was Andrew Horace Victor Pitkethly. By the time he married he had inserted the hyphen. A double-barrelled name sounded posher.

His meanness was best demonstrated during my parents' first Christmas together. They had gone to stay with him for a few days. He had a large mock-Tudor house in Amersham, set in an acre or two of gardens, with a cook, gardener and maids. (In modern terms he'd certainly have been a millionaire.) My mother saw a case of champagne carried in on Christmas Eve and thought a merry time would be had by all. My grandfather managed to drink the lot alone in his study. He was never officially labelled alcoholic – rich men rarely are called that in this country. It's only rich Americans who exult in melodramatic confessions of their weaknesses. "Old Vic" was also in the habit of personally polishing off all the fruit in the garden including vast quantities of strawberries. Very, very occasionally he allowed servants a few battered windfalls from the trees. I've only seen a small photo of him. There was a strong resemblance to George Burns, although he was a little taller, just as my father looked like a life-size version of Charlie Chaplin. Both my father and grandfather were good comics in their way.

In spite of his Guinness Book of Records meanness and the lousy writing-style I feel I'd have liked Vic. He was a wonderfully witty talker and a good gardener. He was also very able with his hands. He could have been a forger. He carved an authentic-looking Elizabethan bed for himself and was a very tolerable amateur painter. On one occasion he added dozens of tiny figures to a Christmas card in watercolour. He'd keep showing it to my mother or the servants, every time he put in another half dozen skaters. "This card was wonderful value," he'd say. "Just look in that corner. I never saw those figures before. Oh yes, and now I can see one up on the roof." Eventually my mother worked out what was happening when the picture was as full as the average Brueghel.

My grandfather was friendly with "Old Wade", the editor of London Opinion. Wade had retired earlier and suddenly started to take an interest in growing rhubarb. Vic was only working in London three days a week by then. He'd play jokes when his train passed Old Wade and his rhubarb in Rickmansworth. On one occasion he dressed up with a cocked hat made from his newspaper, stuck a penny in one eye and concealed one arm behind his back like Nelson. He was in his late sixties at the time. I don't know quite what the other commuters in the First Class compartment made of it all.

Vic's death in 1956 enabled my father to move from Harrow to a large Victorian house in Ealing. For my first few years there we were reasonably prosperous before everything started to go down hill. My father fell out with his brother over the inheritance. There had been a clean split down the middle. Uncle Andrew got Vic's house and antiques while Dad got the cash. Andrew, a firm believer in primogeniture, believed he should have got the lot. He celebrated after the funeral by burning a selection of my father's possessions that were still about the place, including one boot out of a pair of heavy army ones. For some obscure reason I found the idea of one boot being burned deeply distressing as a child. I have always hated wanton destruction of property but still can't fathom why I found this so upsetting. Perhaps it had something to do with my inborn sense of symmetry – two shoes to be burnt or nothing. Or perhaps, it seemed to symbolise something far greater than the relatively small amount one good leather shoe was worth.

Chapter Two: Moving

MY FATHER HAD gone ahead with the removal men to get the furniture laid out. Although he was not remotely artistic in the sense of being able to draw, he had good taste in architecture and furnishings. Being brought up in a place full of antiques educated that into him. The previous owner of our new house, a canny spiritualist landlady called Mrs. Quinlan, sold him some heavy furniture, a few items of which had been in the house almost since it was built. The first owner of the house had been a Cabinet minister called James Round. His taste ran to heavy mahogany wardrobes. The one my father took for himself had three sections. The side parts were full of drawers and the middle was for hanging clothes. It was soon filled with my father's Harris tweed suits and the strange velvet or linen vestments that he used for his chief hobby – getting dressed up as a bishop and taking services with other like-minded friends. I liked to rifle through all the different materials and textures. The side drawers, as well as shirts, were stocked with things my father would let me play with – a vast collection of military buttons, a few dozen lead soldiers, frog feet, a gas mask and the one remaining army boot from Uncle Andrew's act of arson.

My mother and I followed my father in a taxi. Creffield Road was a pleasant suburban street full of large houses, most of them with trees in the front garden – lilacs, magnolia, and flowering cherries. It was also near a large common full of chestnut trees. Landladies who let out rooms or catered for bed and breakfast owned most of the houses.

When we reached the new house all my toys were laid out to greet me. Some were on the sofa; others were on chairs at the table, waiting to be served. There was Ikey (short for Ichabod), a rather revolting doll with a pink fabric body and a decidedly sallow screwed-up little face. He was meant to be a baby doll but looked more like a nasty, discontented old man. I preferred my bears. There were the larger ones, Lord Teddy and Lady Teddy. In time I gave them a family of four children when other little bears were bought for me. Lady Teddy had a taffeta satin red dress. Lord Teddy was unclothed except for a pullover at that stage, but later acquired tartan trousers and a Scottish personality. When I was old enough to know the facts of life I made him the hero of series of perverse scenarios. I cast myself as Birkett, QC, defending him on a variety of rape and murder charges. Threads from his telltale tartan trousers were found on bushes near the scene of the crime, but I always managed to find a rational explanation for this. My mother went along with this game and never ticked me off. She recognised, realistically, that it made a good training for my powers of deduction.

My other toys were Bess, a washed-out bunny with plastic goggling eyes that rolled, Rose, a little pink and white bear that I loved for years, a white woolly dog or two and a nasty little home-made bear, cobbled together from a worn red glove. I didn't even bother to dignify the latter with names. There was also a clockwork bear that you could wind up with a key. He was made out of tin covered in brown cloth. He was probably always slightly faulty. For a few turns of the key he'd execute a wambling walk, teetering from leg to leg. Sometimes he'd deviate to the right, other times to the left. Noticing this propensity I eventually used him as an oracle to give yes or no answers to questions.

The house had a bigger garden than that in Lance Road. In September it was crammed with roses, Michaelmas daisies and golden rod. There were also a number of blackberry bushes, raspberries and loganberries against the wire fence and down at the end where the lawn tailed out and all the plants merged into an unholy mess. There were three main trees, a pear, a Bramley and a Worcester. To my delight they were already laden with half-ripe fruit.

I went at the berries like a demon. I had to be warned off the woody nightshade at the end, but I admired the beauty of its purple and yellow flowers. In the years that followed I acquired an interest in botany that has lasted all my life. My mother was thrifty and set to making all the berries we could not eat into jam. The pantry was lined with bramble jelly. And there were endless blackberry and apple tarts that autumn.

We met our neighbours soon after moving in. We became friendly with the Smiths, or "Lady Smith" and "Man Smith", as I christened them. Lady Smith was a very proper landlady, but fortunately she liked children. Her son, Man Smith, though coming up to middle age was used as her errand-boy. It seemed patently obvious that he would never marry. Occasionally we had outings in their car, a prospect I dreaded. The doors were draughty and the inside smelt strongly of petrol. The outings were always to Richmond Park or Heathrow airport. By the time we got there I always felt ready to throw up.

On the other side there was another landlady, Mrs. Deall. She was less friendly, particularly in later years when our cats started eating her birds. Several years later she called one of my Manx cats "a great ugly brute" for which I stood in the garden and sang a few rousing verses of "Blackbird pie for dinner". Her gardener, Bob, did not appreciate her manner either. He'd retire to the end of his vegetables and mutter: "Old faggot. Who the hell does she think she is? Do this, Bob. Do that, Bob. Old faggot." Then he'd spit. I used to love listening out for this routine as a kid. Mrs. Deall remained blissfully unaware of his thoughts about her.   Mrs. Deall's dour manner was the result of losing her daughter from cancer. It was years before we discovered this. We would certainly have felt more for her if we had known.

On the other side of the road there was a woman whose husband worked for the BBC. I christened her "The Blue-haired fairy" after a character in a little child's version of Pinocchio

I had few books at this stage. Those I remember were some cat-shaped ones with a miaow button hidden in the cover. I pretty soon discovered that they could be hidden under the carpet for visitors to step on. To my disappointment, most people were singularly unperturbed when they heard a strangled miaow coming from the centre of the floor. I was also given three pop-up German fairy storybooks. I particularly liked the scene from Sleeping Beauty where the cook lambasted a scullion with a ladle that could be waggled to and fro by pushing a tab at the side. These books were a gift from Uncle Andrew in one of his rare good moods. I have them still. I was a careful kid who never mistreated books or toys.

Uncle Andrew also decided that we ought to have a cat. He was tired of his aged deaf tabby, Bish, so one day he packed it in an orange-box and sent it to us. He was now living on a farm outside Newport. He usually had a liaison going with one or other woman. He favoured rich married ones who were unlikely to "trap" him. Presumably owning a cat with slight bladder problems had ruined the ambience with his girlfriend of the moment.

My father only heard Bish was on his way when he got home from work. He had to turn round, tired and unfed, to go to Paddington to collect him. I hope it was just thoughtlessness not outright cruelty on the part of my uncle, but the cat had come from Newport without food and water and had been left for hours in the station. I was allowed to stay up late for the arrival of Bish. To be honest I didn't entirely take to him. He was too old to make new friends. My parents once heard me mutter: "You respectable old cat!" to him. "Respectable" has never been a term of endearment in my vocabulary. My father switched his affection to him, or so I thought. Dad seemed to be able to be demonstratively affectionate to just one person or animal at a time. First it was my mother, then me, then the cat. I used to shout: "Pu' Bish down and pi' Fi up!" and burst into tears when he cuddled and stroked the newcomer.

Bish resisted most of my games. My parents came in to see books all over the floor and assumed I'd thrown them at him. That was not so though. I'd seen a picture of Stonehenge and was trying to make a kind of circle of cromlechs from the largest tomes for the cat to pass through. Needless to say he would not oblige. I was rather obsessed with the cromlech form. Another game involved propping two grey twill cushions on a chair covered with the same material and hiding inside like a barrow wight with another smaller cushion to conceal my face.

Within two years Bish had died of old age. I was to become an ailurophile only with the arrival of later cats.

Chapter Three: Demon Pigeons and Bishops

FROM THE EARLIEST age I liked to use toys or objects in a variety of different ways. I was caught climbing out of my playpen at a few months old even before I could walk properly. I had rolled and shoved it next to a sofa, then piled up toy tins into a series of steps to get me out and over the top. A little later, old horsehair mattresses became slides draped over the end of my parents' bed. The bed was actually two singles pushed together. It was one of the ex-Quinlan purchases and possibly also ex-James Round. It was so hellishly uncomfortable that I'm surprised it did not ruin my parents' marriage. The ends and heads were solid slices of mahogany. I could trace demonic faces in the pattern of the wood. Both beds had cast iron frames and box mattresses topped by thinner ones stuffed with horsehair and covered with blue and grey striped ticking. The horsehair had organised itself into large lumps and each bed had a differing sag in the centre. While sex could be had on either half, I suppose, there was no possibility of a cuddle in the middle without a rapid descent into one or other crater.

Another of James Round's wardrobes graced the room. My mother had a wonderful collection of hats inside, left over from the last War – the stage of life when she had been at her dressiest. I loved trying on the big ones – heart-shaped black felt soft as a cat's belly fur, deep yellow coarse straw, fine black straw. She kept her sanitary towels, Doctor White's, at the bottom of the wardrobe. For years I managed to persuade myself that they were hammocks for mice.

The room had a picture of the Tabernacle with all the tribes of Israel camped in the wilderness. I always admired its detail set against the translucent light blue of the walls. Early emulsions had a transparent fresco-like quality that has been completely lost in the thick acrylic modern paints. There was also a print of the head of Venus from the Botticelli picture. It had been given to my mother by her former boyfriend, Louis, a Greek Cypriot who had been born in Paphos. And there were two small framed postcards of the Dürer hare and some Hans Hoffmann squirrels.

My parents picked up another good item of furniture for that room from a Steptoe-style antique shop in Acton. It was an old rosewood spinet that had been converted into a desk with two drawers and a central flap under its flat top. My mother kept armfuls of old underwear stuffed into it – white satin, peach cotton and black lace. I have always had a problem persuading her to part with bras that are decades past their usefulness. Some of these, like the hats, dated from the War. Unlike the hats they hadn't stood the test of time. One day the drawerful of sagging bras got jammed and the handle fell off and disappeared under the carpet. Being a lateral-minded kid I threaded string through the hole left by the handle and harnessed my rocking horse to the drawer. A few rocks and it was open again.

My mother and father were passably off, comfortable anyway, at this stage. My mother often dreamed of buying me wonderful toys like a proper wooden rocking horse rather than the small fur fabric and tin one, or a large dolls' house. My father simply dreamed of giving up work and devoting himself to his strange ecclesiastical hobby. These dreams were never to materialise. Within a few years he was out of a job and we began a gradual descent into penny-pinching poverty.

But for the moment things were still reasonably good. My father went to work as early as he could so that he could leave by four and be home to play with me at teatime. My mother hinted this would not do him any good professionally and she was right. But probably the thing that did him most harm as a journalist was being teetotal. In literary life I've found that while negotiating a contract or meeting to discuss an idea, drinking level with the boys is con-sidered a necessary part of the deal. About the only thing that might get you off is pretending that you'd had a hard night the day before.

When Dad came home one of our favourite games was doing a milk round. I had a little cart on wheels with half a dozen wooden bottles. Some coloured plastic bottles were added to make the game go on longer. Dad would invent occupants for the rooms, treating them like houses. We knocked every door and shouted: "Milko!" Those with cats got extra pints, or cream instead of milk. But the delivery I enjoyed most of all was to the old man who needed six pints a day because he liked to wash his wooden leg in milk.

Dad also installed his train set in a tiny room. He was a terrible carpenter, but this effort was not too bad by his standards. The shelf that ran around the room at adult shoulder-level was only slightly skewed. Dad had several old carriages and engines running on a

mass of track with points that could be changed. A dado strip of
wallpaper with a landscape set the scene together with a few minia-
ture plastic trees. The whole thing was supposed to have been done
for my benefit but it was mostly Dad who played with it. Mum
would catch him at odd times of the day, holding an engine in his
hand, murmuring: "Peep, peep!"

Dad's chief asset as a playmate was his ability to invent bizarre
stories, or the beginnings of them. My favourite stories at this time
were about a pigeon. My father gave the opening lines: "Belinda the
demon pigeon of Acton lived on a gargoyle overlooking a church-
yard..." He often lost patience and let my more disciplined mother
tell the endings. He also invented wonderful names for people. One
of his stories involved a couple living on a barge. They were called
Roderick Ramshackle and Emmeline Mohair. Sometimes the names
he invented for real people turned out to be right. "I bet she's got a
boyfriend called Serge," he said about one woman only to find out
later that it was so. Similarly he labelled an American lady Beulah
correctly. Names were always a source of wonder and amusement to
him. I think they were part of the reason he enjoyed corresponding
with other like-minded 'bishops' around the world. Frequently he
made up rhymes about people. Most were scurrilous. If I was frightened at night I'd be taken into my parents' bed for comfort. I'd lie
on the hard ridge between the two craters. If Mum and Dad were
both sufficiently wide-awake they'd make up rhymes about my
father's correspondents, or give me toned-down versions of limericks like:

There was an old man of Leeds
Who swallowed a packet of seeds.
A lily and rose
Grew out of his nose
And out of his ears grew weeds.

It was years before I heard the real version.

Most Saturdays and every Sunday, strange ecclesiastics would
arrive for tea. There were a few relatively normal people too. These
were normally lonely foreigners who'd been directed to my father
by some mad bishop. Ours was probably the only London address
they had. When the visitors bribed me with sweets or told me stories I was nice to them. Cleaned-up I could look like a little fairy.
God help the visitors though if I got bored. One time I emptied a

tin of emulsion over myself for effect. On another occasion I proudly presented my chamber pot to show what a clever girl I'd been. Frequently also, I said things like: "I don't like him. When's he going?" Then there was the case of sexual harassment...

Moadek was a beautiful young Indian man with the sort of chiselled features I could go nuts about. I followed him to the lavatory demanding a kiss. I even broke in after him when he didn't oblige. His Scottish girlfriend, Elizabeth, didn't take it in good part. She sat and glared at her three-year-old rival for the rest of the afternoon.

Occasionally, if someone my father considered important was coming, I had to be removed to a safe distance. Count Batchinsky and his wife had told us that they were coming to stay with us to discuss the possibilities of opening a Ukrainian Orthodox Church in London. My mother went on strike when she heard the list of demands. They were both strict vegans with bad digestions that required further dietary limitations. Worse still, they demanded absolute quiet and said that they did not like children. My father wasn't too keen on the idea of eating vegetarian, either. We booked them into a local hotel and arranged for them to visit us. I was taken to Clacton to save them from my machinations. Clacton was much more fun. As an added precaution, for days before, the dreary couple were referred to pseudonymously as my parents grumbled and made rhymes about them. My mother took their new name of Maltravers from a Lytton novel. She was afraid that they might still be there when we came back from the sea. (Returning from a day away usually made me either soporific or demonic.) It was a wise precaution – if I should choose to speak ill of Maltravers on my return, the Batchinskys would never know what the Pitt-Kethleys really thought about them...

Chapter Four: I Get Expelled from Sunday School

THE FIRST THING my father had done on entering 11 Creffield
Road, even before setting out my bears, was to select a site for his
"chapel". He opted for the back attic, a large room with sloping
walls and a tiny window that looked down on the garden. In no time
at all it was furnished to his liking with a blue carpet, an altar
designed by a friend and various crosses. The altar cross was wood-
en with carved boulders at its feet. This and a small stone Celtic
cross, a souvenir from Scotland, were my favourites. I liked to run
my hands across them, feeling their different textures and tempera-
tures. In this way I became conscious early on of the inherent ici-
ness of stone. My father also had a bottle of holy water and a tiny
phial of rose-oil chrism. I liked to sniff the latter. There was something faintly desecrational and compelling about touching these
sacred things.

In time the walls were filled with pictures: reproduction icons
and a couple of oil paintings by a "real artist". When I trained at Art
School I ended up despising the latter and finding all sorts of tech-
nical faults in the way Miss Boyagin, an Armenian, had applied her
oils. My father yearned to have a portrait of a minor Russian saint
who had tamed a bear. My mother was reasonably good with water-
colours and was cajoled into promising to do him one. The years
went by and the picture was never started, let alone finished. A saint
alone would have been no problem, but she had grave doubts about
her ability to paint bears. She should, I suppose, have got Lord
Teddy to model for her, with or without his tartan trousers. At one
stage, she even conceived the idea of doing a collage with a piece of
fur representing the bear. But where would she get the piece of fur?
In those days she had never visited a jumble sale and charity shops
had not been invented. She deferred the picture-making while she
waited for one of her fur collars to drop to pieces. Somehow they
were never quite bad enough to be cut up...

The chapel became the setting for a number of services, during
which my father was ordained into literally dozens of strange sects.
Sometimes, too, he would do the ordaining. Some of the bishops he
became friendly with gave him wonderful scrolls and certificates
covered in gold leaf. After the bishops had ordained each other
there was usually a general taking of photographs. One or two of

the Americans had better equipment and would use a flash to do this
in the chapel. Others would take photographs with primitive Box
Brownies in the back garden. I don't know quite what the neighbours made of it all. The bishops, in their robes, would stand
halfway down the lawn, usually on the slightly marshy bit that
sometimes sprouted fairy ring champignons. The photographer
would back up against the square rotary washing-line in order to fit
the whole scene in.

I felt a certain dislike of the guests, especially those who ventured into the garden. They were infringing my territory. I enjoyed
weaving between the sheets in the square maze made by the full
rotary drier. I also liked to run and jump on the grass. Worst of all
I hated them entering my fairy ring. That seemed like a desecration.

At that stage I believed fully in fairies and ghosts, the whole
gamut of them. 11 Creffield Road was just the sort of place to be
haunted. Mrs. Quinlan had been under the thumb of a lodger, a
medium who went under the name "White Eagle". While the
atmosphere in the back attic was tranquil, that in the front was
decidedly iffy. A highly intelligent cat I owned later refused utterly
to enter the room and would bristle all over if I tried to carry him
in. When I slept there in my teens, the bed seemed to vibrate all by
itself. I was too religious at that stage to vibrate it in any other way.
Added to all that, most of the wiring in the house was extremely old.
It probably dated back to the invention of electricity. That in the
pantry was so faulty that it frequently produced an effect like a ball
of lightning when it was switched on. Across the years I accrued
more than my fair share of electric shocks.

My father bought most of the old light fitments from Mrs.
Quinlan. Those in the attics were small opaque glass shades painted with little blue birds. I still have one of them. In other rooms
there were heavy glass globes and in three rooms there were fantas-
tical ornaments. The "Neddy Room" – so-called because I kept my
toy horses in there – was lit by a fitment that had two pink glass
shades on a gilt apparatus that could be lowered with weights for
cleaning. Those on the landing and in the hall were similar but
white and less romantic. The one in the hall seemed to cast heavy
shadows that added to the mystery of the house.

I was three or so when I first began to talk about "The Baba".
My parents assumed I had invented an imaginary friend, as I did not
have many real children to play with. In Harrow there had been sev-

eral children in the road. Although most were older, there had seemed to be more possibilities for play. Most of the people in Ealing seemed to be well-to-do forty-somethings. Children were a rarity. Acton had plenty, but Mum, being slightly snobbish, kept me well escorted and away from these kids. Years later, I enjoyed plumbing the depths of the Acton parks to find out what sexual activities went on and what scams were in operation. Children who lived near the edge of the law were actually more fun to hang out with. But at three, I had to be content with occasional visitors like Jenny and Vivvy, a terminally boring pair with perfectly plaited hair.

The Baba, I told my mother, taught me all sorts of things and talked to me for hours. Perhaps I was displaying a sample of her wisdom one day when my mother was in the throes of making apple tarts for the benefit of some bishop or other. She gave me a spare lump of pastry to play with to keep me out of mischief. I shaped several snakes out of it and laid them down. Then I talked for half an hour non-stop of living in a village in the middle of a lake. The place was a farm, I said, surrounded by a fence of trees cut down the middle. We made cakes in this shape, I told her, to keep the serpents away and to keep us from harm. We baked them on stones. I was very young at the time and unable to read. My mother was conscious that I had never been exposed to any literature either about sympathetic magic or lake-dwellers. The way in which I gave this little talk was adult and sensible. Neither of us was ever able to find any explanation that would fit accepted rational thought.

There was one other inexplicable event. One day, my mother saw me toddling up the stairs towards what seemed to be another figure. She didn't want me to climb too high. Besides, at the top of the house there was a small room with dangerous uncovered water-tanks. If I continued up several flights I might even reach these. As she was about to lunge forward to grab me she looked at the other figure. It was also me, or very like me, but a much older version of the person I was. By the time I was eight or so, I had grown into the other child she had seen, with thick brown hair. Who or what was *The Baba*? A Victorian ghost, something left over from the more recent Quinlan séances, my astral body or my daemon? Or was she merely a trick of light, a mutual hallucination in the shadows of the dark hall?

I had been good as gold until I was christened. My parents had

joked that I didn't like saying goodbye to my friend, the devil. In
reality I was probably a bit pissed off at the decidedly generous dol-
lop of water suddenly dropped on my head by the vicar. From then
on my behaviour deteriorated rapidly. Perhaps it was simply a reaction to all the Christian excesses around me, but there were times
when I definitely showed diabolical leanings. My mother occasionally read me Bible stories, the more colourful ones. Even at three I
began to realise that both Jews and Christians discriminated against
other religions. While my father pursued his aim of drawing all the
Christian religions together into one ecumenical movement I had
other ideas. I felt particularly sorry for the God Baal. I reckoned he
had a raw deal so I decided to reinstitute his worship. By then I had
three toy horses – the rocking one, another fur fabric one on wheels
and a coloured tin one. Their flat broad backs would make ideal
altars, I believed, so I lined them up under our large dining table in
the Neddy Room and poured little oblations to my chosen god –
cinnamon, mixed spice and flower petals. My mother's amusement
was tinged with perturbation. She had grown up as a member of the
ultra-strict Plymouth Brethren in Swansea. Her father was still an
itinerant preacher doing the rounds in Wales and Devon, while her
mother paid frequent visits to the workhouse bearing gifts of food
and Woodbines. Every single generation in her family had yielded
a preacher, back to William Williams of Pantycelyn, the famous
Welsh hymnwriter, and perhaps further back still. Nothing like this
had happened in her family before. I was immediately dispatched to
Sunday School in Acton.

Mum laid on an especially good tea for when I came back on a
Sunday afternoon. She reckoned that if she built up a large open fire
and laid a table full of cakes, tarts and tiny kid-sized pink blanc-
manges surrounded by cherries, that I'd come to associate the party
atmosphere with religion and going to church.

Within a few weeks I suffered the ignominy of expulsion. A rag-
ing Miss Snelgrove demanded that I be taken away. She would not
say what I had done. Back home my parents got the story out of me.
Miss Snelgrove, a florist who specialised in funeral wreaths for a
local undertaker during the week, was a rather an unattractive
woman from a malicious little kid's point of view. Her legs were far
too short for her long body. Towards the end of Sunday afternoon
she would close the class by getting us to process behind her to the

strains of "Onward Christian Soldiers" played loudly by her girl-friend on the piano. Her body bent forward and she sometimes locked her hands behind her back, waggling her thumbs. Virtually every florist, and certainly all wreath-makers, end up with damaged fingertips from pressing the wire into place with the fleshy parts of the thumb and index finger. Children see adult faults in lurid exaggerated detail. Following behind her in file, I found her short-legged body irresistibly duck-like. The mottled horny thumbs even looked like tail feathers down on my eye-level. It wasn't long before I was walking like a very bandy duck too and the rest of the file of kids was sniggering loudly.

My father was angry and muttered something about "the old bitch". Mum was slightly relieved in some ways. While I was not entirely cured of Baal worship, at least I need not mix any more with the Acton kids or risk picking up Miss Snelgrove's less than perfect accent.

Of course, my father was in a way responsible for my imitation. I admired all his bad habits intensely at this stage. Sometimes, when we were out together, he would follow a dog down the road and cock his leg at a lamppost behind it. If he'd seen a duck-like woman before him he wouldn't have been able to resist...

Chapter Five: Uncle Gordon and the Octopus

AT FOUR I took a last ride in my pram. I was already far too big for it but wanted to savour the old experience of being pushed round the town in state again. My father was easily persuaded. I soon realised my mistake as we juddered over a kerbstone and I was nearly thrown out. It was one of those large old-fashioned prams with a kind of primitive spring suspension that rocks the whole body. I had to sit crunched up under the hood to balance. Anywhere further along and I'd have been tipped out by my own weight.

Dad wheeled me into Acton to his favourite fish and chip shop. Mum had banned him from going there as she feared the owner had TB. "Mr. Punch" as we christened him, was a doleful Italian with a narrow chest and dark shadows under his eyes. He used to cough hollowly as he handed over the food. Having collected our chips we then went on to Tony's ice-cream parlour for a tuppenny cone apiece. Tony's had a bizarre painting left over from the Thirties across their front window. A smiling boy and girl holding cones were skipping down a yellow road to nowhere. There was something seriously dodgy about the perspective and the young girl's hair looked dyed and Marcel-waved like an older film star's.

I ate my cone as I was wheeled on in state. As a final treat on the way back, I was bought a tiny set of cups for my dolls from an old junk shop. But it was a precarious experience. I realised I was now far too old for the pram and must put aside childish things – some of them anyway.

Most Saturdays Dad took me into London or to one of the nearby parks. He had a weekly season ticket, so it was only a matter of buying a child's ticket for me. Sometimes we visited parks where he could have a go on the swings or roundabouts uncriticised by Mum. At other times we visited historic spots and churches in the city. He had a whole series of other ports of call too – butchers and café owners that he seemed to know personally. He'd take me for the "Best sandwich in London". Best meant biggest in his terms. One day we visited Baldwin's in Elephant and Castle, a herbalist's where they served frothing pints of sarsaparilla.

The year was punctuated by a couple of holidays with Gran in Mumbles. Gran lived in a late Victorian terrace house next to a chapel. My cousins showed me how to climb through a window into the ground attached to the chapel next door. Gran had a rather grumpy corgi that didn't take to me. Gran herself I adored. For a while I felt I loved her more than my parents. She never told me off after all. My mother was too dignified to dance with me, but Gran bought me a little plastic kid's record player and frolicked round to "She was coming round the mountain".

Gran was a rounded figure dressed in Marks and Spencer's frocks. She favoured pastel shades of pink and green. There was absolutely no attempt made to doll herself up. She never wore make-up yet men found her attractive even in her old age. It was something about her vivacity.

The Gower Coast was a wonderful playground for a kid. The nearest safe bay to Mumbles was Langland. My cousins or my mother would walk me through the park round the corner and up a piece of woodland filled with wild garlic out on to the road that led to Langland. At other times there were car trips with my Aunt Dorothy to the bays at Caswell or Oxwich.

There were several things in Gran's house that I liked playing with. She had an egg-slicer. The minute I got through the door I would say: "Can I play on Gran's harp?" and I'd pluck the wires and extract a few notes. She also had a piano that I loved to improvise on. Fortunately for her I was a gentle improviser – no crashing Chopsticks, just a series of melancholy minor chords and arpeggios. On top of the piano there was an Edward the Eighth Coronation jug. As if by magic it would play "For he's a jolly good fellow" every time I lifted it.

Gran also had deliveries of soft drinks. I loved dandelion and burdock pop. That was one of the Swansea tastes that couldn't be got easily in London. Another was seaweed called laverbread. I still love the stuff. Few people without Welsh blood can stand the sight of it let alone the taste.

Dad sometimes came along on these trips in the pre-Bish days. He even brought Bish down there once in his basket. It was a nightmare journey. The train was crowded so Bish was put up on the rack. Not long after, an appalling smell filled the carriage. It was not Bish's fault this time. My mother took it on herself to bring him down to check. Then she sniffed me, herself, and last of all, my father. The quiet man opposite, a doctor judging by the address on his immaculate leather case, had turned a queasy shade of green. He ate his sandwiches hanging out of the compartment door for air. Eventually, the source of the trouble was diagnosed. My father had filled the pockets of his tweed suit with some boiled rabbit, the cat's favourite treat. It was either the heaters in the train or my father's hot body that turned it off rapidly. Dad solved the problem by tossing it out of the window. He was remarkably fond of doing things like that in trains. In the years that followed I was taught to lob all sorts of things out of carriage windows, preferably when there was a passing goods train with tempting open trucks.

It was rather hoped that Bish would ingratiate himself with Gran and settle there. They did get on well and all looked set fair for an adoption until he piddled in her kitchen. My father explained that the different layout of the house had confused him. Curiously, he had often been confused at home too.

As well as Bish, Dad had been carrying Jacko, a large evil monkey with a fur fabric body and a rubbery face and hands. The hands had horrible light pink palms that gave my mother the creeps. Gran didn't take a shine to him either, but at least he didn't pee in her kitchen. She had a bit of a thing about the simian species and had obviously made her own bad-minded conclusions on Darwinian evolution. While visiting a small private zoo, Gran looked at a rather bald and sickly monkey and said in sorrowful tones: " Some men are very wicked."

The slightly human Jacko had a similar effect on a lot of women. Years later, I gave him to a neighbour who had a young son. At first the boy played with him happily enough until his mother, who got maniacally active during pregnancy, took against Jacko and threw him on a bonfire. Dad said: "Must have reminded her of her husband."

Gran occasionally came to see us in London with a greenish-black mess of laverbread from Swansea Market in her bag. She would prefer to arrive by coach and Dad would go to meet her in Ealing Broadway to help her with her things. They both had bad feet. My father had not been sent anywhere dangerous in the War because of his extremely flat ones and Gran had corns. Neither of them could walk more than a quarter of a mile. I thought Gran's corns were fascinating and wanted some of my own. Her Carnation Corn Caps were packed so prettily. I liked the little pink rings she stuck in the toes of her stockings to keep her crossover sandals from pressing on anything. At three or four, I also fancied having false teeth and a very large bust.

I was her favourite grandchild at that period. Gran died before I became a champion swearer, something that might well have put her off me. My grandfather, a good-looking man, a bit like a sexagenarian Dennis Waterman, was less keen. "She's a trouble to you," he said disapprovingly to my mother. I had been told he was a wonderful storyteller, yet he wouldn't tell me any. He had got too old to be bothered. My older cousins had heard all his stories. I resented his refusal to tell them to me, so my mother hinted tactfully that they might not have been strong enough for my tastes. He was known for putting good stories into his sermons, so she may well have been right. I was better served with my father's demon pigeon sagas.

Holidays were in Gower, but I also had odd day-trips to the sea. Dad arranged them neurotically. The tickets were purchased in advance and we had to go whatever the weather threw up. Sometimes we waded round towns deep in snow or slush, or battled with a force nine gale. We would be got up horribly early and Mum would turn a whole sliced brown loaf into sandwiches with a tin of Chicken Supreme. Dad would carry bottles of Tizer or made-up squash. We started eating the sandwiches on the tube, long before we got to Charing Cross, Fenchurch or wherever we were starting from. I liked the Chicken Supreme, but the day my parents gave me shaken-up lukewarm Lucozade to wash it down, it was all too much for me. I went into an empty carriage of the Folkestone train and threw up all over the floor. It was literally wall-to wall vomit. All we could do was chuck our newspapers in on it and depart to another carriage. Some drunk probably got the blame.

Once at the seaside I was not always well behaved. Dad liked to dragoon us round a place as fast as possible, eat lunch early, then catch a mid-afternoon train home. It was not always possible to find loos or restaurants when we wanted them. On one occasion I was taken short in the model village at Southsea and pissed in the castle moat.

Lunch on our awaydays was usually fish and chips, or, in my father's case, pies and chips. He was never able to resist a pie in any shape or form. We used to joke that he'd have eaten Kitekat in one. On one occasion he bought a solid plaster demonstration model from a baker's window by mistake and tried to bite into it. When he took it back, much to his delight, he was given a huge pie in recompense.

Dad had a real thing about pies and curries. He would frequently eat them between meals. However much my mother fed him, he could always be seduced by the smell of his favourite foods when he passed a café. There was one occasion when he was lured into an Indian restaurant for a Madras straight after Christmas dinner – a stunt that didn't earn him Brownie points with Mum. At other times my mother would find a host of steak and kidney pie wrappers in the pockets of his suit.

I didn't realise my parents were fat until I was ten or so. At four or five, all adults, small or big, looked like great hulking rounded creatures. I remember feeling an almost Swiftian disgust for the whole species. They were all creatures from Brobdignag. I hated the smell of my mother's powder – "like farts and violets". Although she was always a very clean person I could smell the grease of her skin warming her cosmetics.

While my mother was always having baths, my father preferred to stay filthy as long as possible. In my early years I took after him. Like him, I had to be persuaded, cajoled and implored into taking a bath. I never had any ducks, but I liked to take toys in with me. I had several wheels and balls that my father had bought in a pet shop. They were intended for use by budgies and hamsters. My favourite game, and the only one that could get me into the bath, involved an elaborate fantasy scenario. My father had brought home an enormous bear that we christened Uncle Gordon. He was not particularly handsome or good quality, but he was very large. I saw him as a fearful old man. There was something decidedly unheroic in his expression. We pretended that the house was an old people's home and that Uncle Gordon was about to take his weekly bath. Mum would play the Matron, forcing him to the door. My role was that of an octopus. I had a pair of green goggles on my eyes and a white swimming cap over my mouth and chin. My long wet hair stood in for tentacles. As the fearful bear put his nose round the door he would see a monster emerging from the bath and stutter: "Oh no, M-m-m-m-matron, th-th-th-there's an octopus in the bath." Matron would tell him it was all nonsense, and when they both looked in together, all was returned to normal. We would enact this scene several times until I was reduced to a state of hysterical laughter and could put up with my mother shampooing my hair and soaping me.

Chapter Six: My Pets

BETWEEN THE AGES of four and five, I acquired a paraplegic pet pigeon. I christened her Lucy. There was something wrong that made her unable to fly. It was nothing visible and obvious that could be fixed. Perhaps she had just lost her nerve. We assumed that, sooner or later, she would take off and fly away. In the summer we kept her in a back room on the ground floor. If it was hot, we left the large sash window open so that she could enjoy the fresh air and watch the other pigeons. I gave them all names. Most were Arthurian characters – Galahad, Percival, Guinevere, Lancelot and so on. Lucy soon got herself a boyfriend. We called him Albert because he had a huge swollen pouter chest like a Victorian swell. He was a real pimp of a bird. He regularly came in knocked Lucy over, stole her corn, wallowed in her water and shagged her. I didn't understand about sex, so I read the whole situation as violence. It put me off pigeons for years. I became slightly phobic about them and did not cross Trafalgar Square again until I was eighteen, although, as a toddler I had regularly fed the birds and posed with them. I also felt that pigeons were one item I could retain on my menu at a later stage when I became temporarily vegetarian. I explained to friends in restaurants that I was eating them "out of revenge". They thought I'd been crapped on, but really, I hoped one day to eat that revolting bird, Albert, stewed, roasted, fricasséed, or swimming in cream.

Bish was far too respectable to trouble Lucy. His hunting days were long over. He passed away in his sleep at the grand old age of eighteen. It was about six months before we got another cat. I was taken into London with my father to collect her. We were still at a relatively prosperous stage, so my parents had ordered a pedigree Siamese. We might, they thought, make a little money off her kittens by getting her mated when she was old enough.

I was thrilled by my present. She was lean, lithe and active as a ferret. She was never a lap cat, but sometimes draped herself round my neck like a living, moving fur collar. I called her Tess, after Tess of the d'Urbervilles. I had not read the book at that stage, I still could not read, but I had heard my mother mention it and I took to the name.

Mum was still reading to me. I enjoyed being read to so much that I pleaded and cajoled her into doing it for a great many years.

At five, I had just got into Beatrix Potter. Mum would read a bit out, then show me the illustrations. One incident in *Peter Rabbit* absolutely terrified me. I couldn't bear MacGregor. As an even younger child I had called him "Gegger". I would stare at a blank wall and mutter his name followed by the words: "Uggy man!" It was almost as if I could see someone or something lurking round the house. Very possibly I could...It took months for my mother to find a way of exorcising the "uggy man". In the end she wrote his name on a blackboard and let me wipe it out. Then we burnt the wet cloth we'd used to wipe the name away.

By five, I had a copy of *The Tailor of Gloucester*. I preferred it to *Peter Rabbit* – there were no horrors there. The illustrations seemed like the most beautiful things I'd ever seen. I really coveted the embroidered waistcoat as I was beginning to get a little dress conscious. I had pleaded, unsuccessfully, to have a purple velvet dress for the beach. Mum said later that she was rather sorry she didn't let me have one. I was an odd mix of the essentially female and the tomboy. On the one hand I set myself no girlish limits, on the other, I loved pretty things.

One of my favourite pretty things was an old Flower Fairy book. I found stories about ordinary humans rather boring at this stage. It had to be fairies or anthropomorphic animals. I had several books about Prudence Kitten and Mum had a couple of the Orlando stories. I also adored Rupert Bear. I was fond of him until my twenties, when I forced myself to part with the whole collection. I had been having surreptitious reads of the annuals to a horribly late age.

I took the anthropomorphism of my books into real life. Even now, I attribute all sorts of weird motives to my cat and let him use the computer and try to understand what he writes – it's in code of course. I also have a sneaking sympathy with those who commit acts of bestiality, as long as the animal enjoys it, that is. It seems an understandable, if not a natural urge. I can't understand why some men think it's more okay morally to kill and eat an animal than shag it.

My birthday present, Tess, had beautiful slanting blue eyes. She was a Sealpoint. I began to imitate her cries and purrs and started to kid myself I had mastered cat language. Tess was not a large vocabulary cat. Her instincts were decidedly basic. Her language was limited to two words or phrases: "Arora!" done as loudly as possible and a sotto voce "Miroway!" As she grew into teenage adulthood the *Aroras* got almost unbearably loud. My first assumption was that *Arora* meant "Let me out!" and *Miroway* meant "I love you". Looking back on it I'm inclined to think the meanings were more complex. The first was probably an order: "Get the bloody window open. I want to go out and be shagged", while the second was "I'm going to suck up to you so that I can steal your dinner."

While Bish had not been a pigeon-fancier, Tess was another kettle of fish. The moment she saw Lucy, you could tell that she had decided exactly what she wanted for dinner that evening. We kept them apart for a while, but Tess became good at picking locks. After one episode where she'd terrorised Lucy into a fainting fit we decided to have the pigeon put down. Lucy still couldn't fly after all. My father explained this to the vet and was horrified when he seized her in front of him and wrung her neck. After that he took up with a more expensive vet in central London. At least he had the manners to finish sick animals with more discretion behind the scenes.

After my fifth birthday we had a few months of peace before Tess got set into nymphomaniac mode. She may have had a pedigree that went back to the Conqueror – she was registered as Creffield Lady Tessa – but in practice she had the morals of an alley cat. When she first went on heat we took her to a cattery to be mated. Unfortunately she didn't take to pedigree cats. She left the handsome Bosun in his own corner. When she came home she slithered through two inches of open window and chased after the one who was to become the love of her life, a surly Manx cat who lived in a turret in a house down Wolverton Gardens. He only had one and a half ears and his face was busted in like that of a prizefighter. He was decidedly coarse too. His owner told me that he loved being groomed with a heavy garden broom, then finished off with the vacuum cleaner.

In the January after my birthday I started school. I went into it with an open mind. I even thought meeting other children might have been nice, but I very soon decided that school wasn't – an opinion I was never to change.

I had just begun to learn to read. I had been given some plastic letters in several colours. I'm inclined to think that not having a different colour for every single letter in such sets is a big mistake. Though I'm not dyslexic, I still have an occasional tendency to write

DOG instead of GOD, or vice versa. I like to blame this on the fact
that both D and G were bright green in my set. Of course there may
be other, more sinister explanations.

At Silverdale the work of teaching me to read continued. I
longed to be able to tackle *Farmer Lob*, which was reserved for the
brightest kids. I had nothing against learning, what I really hated
about school was the senseless discipline. One of the teachers decided that we all had to line up every morning at break time to do up
our shoelaces. The last one to do so would be booed. Needless to
say I got booed regularly by all apart from one little boy who fancied me and confided that he hadn't joined in. My mother soon
remedied the problem by fitting me with elastic bootlaces.
Although she was generally supportive of school and teachers she
would occasionally conspire to beat the system. She used tact at
times too. She had brought me up to say lavatory, but the school
preferred the prurient "toilet". She immediately assumed that the
teacher concerned was lower middle class, at best, however she was
sensible enough not to say this at the time. Instead she covered the
situation by telling me that the school ones were toilets, but ours
was a proper lavatory.

At the end of the first term, one of my teachers phoned to say:
"She's been stealing money and we want it back." My mother was
horrified. Stealing was a particularly common crime in her view.
She upended me and my blazer until the "money" all spilled out. To
her great relief it proved to be cardboard money. I had borrowed it
to try to teach myself to count properly in the holidays. I was soon
bought some cardboard money of my own and a toy post office set.
I loved the latter and it started me off on a most bizarre game. I
would sit, three quarters of the way up the stairs, and chuck an enve-
lope down while shouting: "Telegram for Kitchener!" Mum had
told me about the "Kitchener wants you!" adverts and I had taken
to the name. In view of my former preoccupation with *The Baba*,
Mum began to wonder if there wasn't more to this game than met
the eye. Was I perhaps, picking up on something from the past that
James Round, Cabinet Minister, had ordered in that house?

I had always believed in my own worth and importance before
going to school. I had a ready wit that sometimes amazed my parents. When my Mum wouldn't allow me into the bathroom with
her, I shouted, "Open in the name of the Law!" when this failed,

knowing her religious propensities, I changed it to "Open in the name of the Lord!" That kind of ability to use words and make jokes almost as soon as I could speak enthralled some adults. I was used to admiration. As soon as I entered school all that fell away. I was seen as a child who was only beginning to read, beginning to count and who couldn't do up her shoelaces. It was at this stage that I felt I needed to assume another sort of persona and attach a little regal dignity to myself, and so I became fascinated with everything to do with Queen Victoria. I began to identify with her and had my long light brown hair plaited and coiled into earphones. I collected dozens of Victorian coins and would get relatives to give me their old bun pennies, or the later ones where the queen wore a little coronet. I was becoming more and more difficult and would say, "We are not amused!" with increasing frequency. Sometimes my parents even had to sing "God save our gracious queen" before I'd consent to go to bed.

Chapter Seven: School

ALTHOUGH I MASTERED reading and counting reasonably quickly, school became an intolerable burden to me. I had to be bribed to go with little presents of china cats. The worst scam I worked was insisting that I had to walk my puppet, Muffin the Mule, to school. Silverdale was over half a mile away and Muffin the Mule's legs were a good deal shorter than mine. Even walking him down one road could take an hour.

I had become a proper drama queen by then with huge vocal projection. The neighbours made tactful enquiries after hearing me declaim: "No Daddy, please don't do it, Daddy. Oh no, not that, Daddy!" I was not being interfered with, my long-suffering parents had merely suggested an early night.

Dad was very fond of early nights himself. While I didn't notice how early they were as a very young kid, in the years that followed I did. Mum would stay up to ten or eleven, but he was away by eight at latest, sometimes even six or seven. After that the house would begin to rock with a Baroque trumpet concerto of snores. Often there was considerable tunefulness in them. Every hour or so Dad would pop down in a pair of slightly grubby Y-fronts to tell my mother how late it was. Eventually she would give up and join him.

I had persuaded Mum to read me dozens of ghost stories – the whole of M.R. James, a selection of Poe and some Sheridan LeFanu. To be fair to her, she did take a lot of persuading. I may even have intimidated her a little. The Poe was a little too Gothic for me but I loved the others. There was something profoundly creepy about M.R. James in particular. The dry, academic real-life side was drawn so realistically that the supernatural became utterly believable too. In a house lined with several thousand books I could believe in the world of the occult magician. There were comparatively few stories that could frighten me, much as I longed for that frisson of terror. I never had nightmares. A few stories worked for a while. While they worked, I would get off to sleep uneasily watching patches of light that had filtered through some gap in the curtains as they illuminated parts of the wallpaper. By day I was quite fond of this paper. It was a soft, inoffensive lime green with little black line drawings of plants on it. There was also a cuckoo clock in the room made from a self-assembly kit from Switzerland. It had been bought with wedding present money from "Old Wade", Vic's friend. Originally it had graced my parents' room. Dad used to say "Aah!" every time the bird appeared. It was an odd choice for a wedding present in view of all the continental and Elizabethan jokes about cuckoos. Needless to say, Dad had assembled the kit wrong so that the bird popped out upside down and murmured: "Oo Cuck!" It was a source of amusement for years until the weights fell off and the clock was put to rest. I left the weights lying on my cupboard for years. I liked them too. They were heavy lumps of metal moulded in the shape of long brown fir cones.

If M.R. James's *Whistle and I'll Come to You* or Dickens's *The Signal Man* worried me too much I would wander down to my parents' room in what seemed to me to be the middle of the night, but was probably only eleven or twelve. I used to wear my white candlewick bedspread over my head in case I met anything nasty in the corridor. Then I'd climb in on the ridge between my parents. Tess was often already down there if she wasn't in one of her *Arora* phases.

After an early night, Dad was bright as a button at dawn. He would sprint to the lavatory. On cold days he'd shout: "Ruddy Baffinland!" or, "My tiny Nizhni-Novgarod is frozen!" Only recently, while reading Solzhenitzyn, did I realise how funny the latter joke was. Nizhni-Novgorod, apart from being a somewhat frozen place, is best known in Russia as the site of an Orthodox Seminary. Presumably, some obscure Russian or Latvian bishop had told my father of this and he'd immediately connected the word seminary with his penis.

At the weekends Dad usually brought Mum breakfast in bed at weekends, something she did not want. She preferred to get up a little later and make it for all of us. The only thing Dad could cook was sausages. To make sure they were thoroughly cooked he would burn them all over. Mum's breakfast in bed usually consisted of two or three chipolatas that were black as pitch and stuck to the plate with the lard they'd been cooked in. There was usually a glass of tepid lemon barley on the side. Mum couldn't trust him to make tea properly. He was in the habit of sticking a finger down the spout of the kettle to see if the water was boiling. If it passed his test it never was. The long Earl Grey leaves would float around on the surface of the cup. Fortunately for my health, Mum had put a stop to him preparing my baby food after she'd caught him having a swig from one of my bottles and smacking his lips.

Before we got up and joined him, Dad would use his quiet time alone to feed and talk to Tess. He loved cooking for cats. They didn't criticise him like humans did. He used to come back with dreadful gory bargains from Smithfield – a carrier-bag full of lights from some large animal – hearts, lungs etc. all in one tangled mess. He would cook these in a huge pan. They boiled over frequently and the house sometimes stank of them. He liked to break them up by hand while they were still hot. Then he'd wipe his greasy hands on walls, work surfaces and taps. Cleaning up after him was like painting the Forth Bridge. On Saturdays he would buy coley from Mr. Cope, our fishmonger. Like most London fish it was never really fresh. When Tess' leavings got really high they would be thrown out on the lawn however much Mum begged him not to. Sometimes she thought vaguely of returning to work, but realised what a hellhole the house would become if Dad were left to his own devices.

When the mail arrived Dad was at the letterbox like a dog, fielding it as it came through. He always had a good haul. A few years later I collected all the foreign stamps from Ukrainian bishops, Norwegian Metropolitans and South African Archimandrites. Most of what was going on was a secret. I caught the odd glimpse of flashes of gold and red ribbon at the time. After Dad's death, my mother and I were faced with huge document boxes full of ordination and dubious degree certificates. One of his friends even made Dad the Duc d'Eauville. Mum knew about that one at the time, but took her status of Duchess with a pinch of salt.

In the summer, my spell of Purgatory at Silverdale was over before the real hell of Haberdashers' began. I had passed the entrance exam easily. My reading was quite good by then. One of the teachers asked how high I could count. I came out with a vast number like one million, six hundred thousand, five hundred and sixty six, much to her surprise. In my view, you could only count to a number if you had done so aloud. All my spare moments were spent counting aloud to Tess or the birds, or whoever could hear me, and that was as far as I had got...

The chill of autumn had already set in when my mother marched me down Hanger Lane to my new school. It was an unpleasant walk. I found myself choking on the petrol fumes by the time we got to North Ealing. My red blazer and gingham dress had been exchanged for a deep green tunic and blazer and a turquoise blouse. The blouse chafed the sensitive skin on my neck and filled me with rage by the time I arrived. My mother had kitted me out with a woollen vest underneath it all. My early days seem to have been one long cycle of itchiness and stifled heat. Years later I self-diagnosed an allergy to sheep's wool. These days I rarely can stand anything but silk next to the skin.

There were fifteen of us in the preparatory school, a sort of bungaloid sports building that was used by the older girls from the main school in the afternoon. Mrs. Young presided over us. She was an elderly Scot with a fiery red face. My mother always believed it had something to do with her being a Baptist deacon. Every Baptist she knew had the same colour complexion.

My one act of rebellion against Mrs. Young consisted in writing the odd comment on her, scratched in the dust in the manner of Jesus when the woman was taken in adultery. To make sure she could not read the words I transliterated them into Anglo Saxon runes. I had learnt to write these from a small pictorial history book about the Saxons. My mother teased me by saying that Mrs. Young probably understood these quite well as the average English course included some Anglo Saxon. I felt a little nervous about this until I established that (a) Mrs. Young had only been to a training college, and (b) English courses might include Saxon but did not include runes. I enjoyed the power of having a secret code. My act was probably inspired too, by my favourite M.R. James story, *The Casting of the Runes*.

Two or three years ago, Suzie Mackenzie interviewed me for the *Guardian*. Knowing that Haberdashers' had a fairly large proportion of Jewish girls she asked: "Did you have trouble with the Jewish Mafia?" I said no, quite truthfully, and told her that it was the Scottish Mafia I had problems with. Moments later I realised that Mackenzie is a thoroughly Scottish name. Unfortunately, there was some truth in my claim. Mrs. Young disapproved of me on sight. Every day the Scottish mothers of a couple of the girls would come and pour a little more poison in her ear about me. Little Isobel, had been frightened by my ghost story-telling, they complained. I was blamed for the fact that she had nightmares. Isobel had in my mother's opinion been rendered a nervous wreck by her mother spending months away "convalescing" without even sending her a post-card. But Mrs. Young always sided with the Scots... I had trouble also from another Scottish child. Catriona had the loveable habit of waddling round on her knees and kicking other children up the bum during prayers. Mrs. Young's eyes were always so tightly closed that she never noticed this until myself or some other kid yelped with pain. By the time her eyes were open Catriona was miraculously back in place.

Preparatory school was a constant round of physical pain. There was a hard core of embryo torturers who had developed special kicking, scratching or pinching techniques. In another culture they'd have gone on to join the SS. My having long hair in plaits may have delighted my father, but it gave the torturers something to catch hold of. I can't pretend I was a saint, of course, but I don't believe I usually started the violence. My preferred method was melodramatic words. I would move towards another girl who'd offended me declaiming: "I'll strangle you!" Like those of the hero of some horror film (not that I'd seen any) my hands would twitch in the air with a life of their own. It was enough to send some little girls into hysterics. My mother was sent for again and again. Mrs. Young was developing a firm belief in my psychopathic tendencies even though my threats were only threats and I left no visible marks. Her opinion was further confirmed when I did a picture of a murder complete with lots of red in a painting lesson and also pro-fessed a liking for the unadulterated more violent older versions of one or two fairy tales.

I was now quite a good reader. Mrs. Young had copies of Farmer Lob, but when I got to it I found it quite babyish and infinitely beneath me. I learnt a kind of lesson from that. If you don't get the things you want or pray for when you want them, when you do, they often seem empty and worthless. By six I was able to read adult books. My mother read *The Lion, the Witch and the Wardrobe* to me. I enjoyed it so much that I promptly collared it and read it again to myself. It was my first proper book. Even now I retain a nostalgic affection for it. It was an entirely appropriate book for me. There was all the anthropomorphism I could wish for, together with a sense of pagan mythology. I was drawn to all the half-breed crea-tures, the fauns and centaurs, etc. It was to be part of a lifetime attraction to the mixing of the human and divine, or the human and bestial, and the existence of parallel worlds, cultures within cultures. In the years that followed I grew to realise what an outsider I was and this affinity grew even stronger.

Chapter Eight: Little Girls' Parties

SCHOOL WAS FOR the morning only four days a week. At lunchtime I would make the return journey down Hanger Lane with Mum. Sometimes, a Polish friend, Karen Fielder, went alongside on her huge red tricycle, which was built like a tank. I used to have to jog to keep up with her.

One afternoon a week we were all marched down Twyford Avenue to the main school. A trainee teacher, Susannah, took charge of us. We all liked her. Our tendency was to prefer young teachers unless the old ones were spectacularly kind to us. We used to arrive in time for lunch. Mrs. Young had informed us how nutritious and well-balanced school meals were. It was a point that would be rubbed in by later teachers. There was a kind of hidden implication that we were all fed on shit at home. Because we were there on the same day each week, school dinners were fairly constant. The part we liked was the dessert. It was almost always squares of rice crispies congealed together with melted chocolate. The first course was usually fish fried in breadcrumbs, a stewed tomato and grey boiled potatoes. The fish was even less fresh than Mr. Cope's was, but it was the tomato I found really offensive. It was the first of many occasions when I begged my mother to write a note to have me excused from one or other food item. Every crumb of a school dinner had to be eaten. Haberdashers' had an inflexible rule about it. We were all watched to make sure every nauseous mouthful went down. This meal was relatively inoffensive compared with some we were expected to eat in the coming years. Quite why any school should consider it morally valuable to force kids to eat every morsel of things that disgust them I have never been able to understand. Surely, in adult life, it's a man or woman's taste and discrimination about food and other things that mark him out from the beasts. Yet, in the years that followed we were supposed to feast and be grateful for whatever nasty slop or overcooked titbit was set before us. Every scrap of fat on the meat was supposed to be eaten in the cause of discipline and "good nutrition", likewise lumps of black in potatoes that had gone bad.

At home I was allowed much more freedom about what I ate. My diet was fairly healthy. I was brought up on brown bread and fresh home cooking. I've never really been able to stand anything else since. Looking back at what I ate from a modern more health-conscious point of view, all that was wrong with my diet was a rather high fat content and the sheer quantity. Home dinners were like an eating competition. Dad would shovel down a second helping so I felt I had to have one too. The fact that I was six and less than a third of his weight didn't deter me.

At school I was never really tempted to overeat. Lunch was something to be got through. Afterwards, for that first term, the Scripture teacher got us making items for the Korean Sale, an annual charity fete in aid of some orphans adopted by the school. It was a kind of craft fair where all of us kids were expected to buy back the crap we had made. At six, we were only let loose on small pottery objects like candleholders, folded blotters stitched up the middle and felt-covered flannel needle-cases. Haberdashers' believed in forcing us to be charitable. We were also taught to knit bulging baggy squares for the form blanket, which was displayed in all its hideous glory at "Dorcas".

Our other autumn ordeal was learning carols for the end of term service. Everything had to be memorised so that there would be no rustling of pages. Fortunately the Preparatory was only expected to learn a few. I was quite fond of one of our pieces. It started: "From out of a wood did a cuckoo fly". Then we all did a couple of cuckoos. Another verse had a pigeon that went "Tsucroo". I've completely forgotten what the other bird was. It was fun for kids though – a bit like an upmarket, religious version of *Old Macdonald had a farm*. There was one part of the Carols ordeal that I did not find at all amusing. The preparatory form had to troop on to the school platform and stand on its edge for their songs. When you're less than four feet six, standing on the edge of a platform of much your own height is no laughing matter. At that stage I was certainly acrophobic. In the years that followed I acquired several more phobias. By my late teens I decided to deal with each and every one of those fears separately. By that stage I was on a Goethe-like pursuit of the goal of Classicism. Every weakness in myself had to be eliminated. I had ceased to find anything attractive in the Victorian, romantic image of fainting womanhood. I knew that adult life would demand resourcefulness and strength and that these were positive goals to work towards.

After doing our handwork for the Korean Sale the other lesson in our afternoon at the main school was Dancing. My mother didn't sign me on for the first term. She had been a fat clumsy child and had managed to avoid dancing all her life. Although I was neither fat nor clumsy, she assumed I'd hate it too. By the second term I'd persuaded her to let me have a go. We had to have a coloured tunic sewn to a special pattern. Haberdashers' was great on forcing mothers to be involved in making odd garments for different activities. Most of the mothers were stay-at-home housewives. The school would never have been able to enlist such unpaid co-operation in worthless tasks otherwise. I chose lilac for my tunic. I thought I looked like a fairy and enjoyed prancing around in it. Dancing was done either barefoot or in red ballet shoes. Miss Parker taught us. In summer she taught Swimming. In her youth she had won a diving medal in the Olympics. Although she was near retirement age she had kept her youthful figure. Unfortunately it was combined with an old fisherman's face, not that her girlfriend seemed to mind.

Most of us liked Miss Parker. She was less righteous than Mrs. Young was. She had a kind of old-fashioned, jolly-hockey, Angela Brazil attitude as she hurried us along. Being bossed by her was reassuring. We knew she didn't mean ill. It was a very different case with some of the other teachers whose hands we were to pass through in later years.

On my sixth birthday, or rather the Saturday nearest to it, I had a party. As there were only fifteen girls in the Preparatory, it was simpler and kinder to invite the lot, friends and enemies alike. I already had a discreet blue wool party dress from Bentalls with red velvet ribbon and diamanté trimming. We were still at the stage where we could afford to buy clothes. To my mother's chagrin I demanded a nylon party dress too, after finding that it was all in vogue in other kids' parties. She gave in eventually and told me that mine was an extra special nylon. Those with a figured raised pattern, she felt, were a little less common than a plain see-through colour. Mine was turquoise with a kind of jacquard effect in white. By nylon standards it was relatively subtle. My mother judged some of my friends as common on sight, particularly those who arrived in poorer quality nylon.

Little girls are far vainer than the vainest of adult women. It's difficult to convey the full horror of the all-girls party to those who have not experienced it themselves. About half the girls who attended had already decided they were going to be the best dressed, the one who won most prizes and the one who screamed loudest. "Here comes trouble!" thought my mother as they flounced through the door. Yet this party was by far the least violent of all I had. The girls had not yet got into the full swing of devilry.

Tea was successfully negotiated after a game or two. My mother had prepared quantities of sausages on sticks, tiny crustless sandwiches – ham for the Gentiles, tinned salmon, chicken supreme or fish paste for the Jews. There were tiny fairy cakes covered in hundreds and thousands, coconut beehives and individual jellies in cardboard dishes shaped like flowers. They had fruit cocktail set in them and one or two kids turned squeamish at the sight, fearing it might be something worse. My father had prepared jugs of orange and lemon squash, though my mother had insisted on doing the rest. She didn't want black sausages or finger-tested foods.

After tea, Dad pretended to be Charlie Chaplin and somersaulted over our Egyptian leather pouffé. Some of the kids laughed hysterically. The humourless ones just glared. Things had gone relatively well till then. Afterwards we played shipwreck in my bedroom. It was never quite the same again. Several girls used the bed as a trampoline to get the wind to huff up their nylon skirts. Others queued in my old white cot until the springs gave with a sad twang. After that it was time to go home and parents started to arrive. Everyone was given a parting present to console the losers – ballpoints, rain hats, coloured combs, etc. By then a few fights had broken out – rivalries over whose nylon was fullest – and a few departed red with rage or full of tears.

Virtually every Saturday for the first two terms, someone had either a birthday or a Christmas party. Those who were richest hired conjurers. They never impressed me, although, these days, I like watching elaborate illusions on TV. Most of the ones we saw just did a few small tricks – joining bits of rope, making small items disappear, or making fools of us by handing over a floppy wand. There were never even any rabbits in their hats and the last thing a little monster of vanity wants is a wand that flops. Conjurers left us all completely cold.

My mother made discreet enquiries from me on what other girls' houses were like. As my parents didn't drive, other fathers or mothers often brought me home. I didn't have enough of an eye for

detail to remember everything to report back to Ma. All she usually got out of me was some admission that the other house was smaller than ours, or that the bedrooms didn't have washbasins.
Occasionally an irate parent would bring me back with claims I'd
wrecked the party. My mother took all this with a pinch of salt,
knowing full well that their particular little demon had done much
the same at mine.

When summer came the party season seemed to be over. I
enjoyed that term more. There was swimming, once a week, at the
main school. I couldn't swim at that stage, but enjoyed taking great
strides with a cork float in one hand and the rope that cordoned off
deeper water in the other. We had old-fashioned swimsuits in aqua-
marine jersey. It became a little baggy when waterlogged. The
straps each had an odd hook fastening. It was supposed to make
them easier to put on, but equally it made them easier to undo, a
fact that embarrassed us years later when we had more to show.

The playing field that stretched into the distance from our
pavilion was more fun in the summer too. I called the end of it,
where the grass was long and unmowed, Halleloopah. It was a kind
of corruption of Halleluiah. Once, I ran up to the end, a banned
area. It was full of beautiful grasses – wild rye, barley and purplish
Yorkshire mist. The field was cordoned off from the road by pol-
larded hornbeams. It was easy to believe I was out in the country.
One of the things I remember most from that age was the feeling of
distance and how tired I became after a walk or a run. Probably, if I
went back there, the field would look a tenth of the size it seemed
to me then. To a six-year-old it was like running a marathon. The
pavilion seemed infinitely far away and looked like a speck in the
distance, and so I was taken short and had to squat down to shit
amongst the long grass. I told the story to my parents after as if one
of my friends had done it. My mother sussed out the lie by the
expression on my face.

Like the "knights of old" in the rhyme, I wiped my "arse on tufts
of grass". Even at that stage I was alive to the beauty of nature and
was beginning to take an interest in botany. I vaguely remember
apologising to the grass I used in lieu of toilet paper. I couldn't help
but see all nature as animate. I particularly believed in trees as
beings and tried to communicate with them as I touched their bark.
I was beginning to be hyperactive and would use their lower

branches as something to swing or somersault on. When given more freedom from parental control I did the same on every bus-shelter and used all the straps and handles in the underground to somersault back or forward. Who needs adventure playgrounds? To adventurous children the whole of life is a playground.

Chapter Nine: Child Guidance

MY PARENTS WROTE a note to get me two weeks off in June for a holiday in the Isle of Wight. It was the second time we had gone there. We never holidayed in hotels. I was not to be trusted in polite company, so it was caravans, or Gran's house in Mumbles. On our first visit we had taken Tess. We had been told that Siamese didn't mind going out for a walk on a lead. We tried it at Bembridge but Tess had other ideas and simply crouched down in her blue harness and refused to budge.

The caravan camp was at St. Helen's. We went there three summers running until we made the place too hot to hold us with Tess and six kittens packed into the small caravan. After that, my parents decided to holiday separately. Dad was left alone with the cats. When I was older I sometimes got two holidays – the long one with Mum and the odd weekend with Dad. Mum hated having a caravan full of cats to cope with. She considered it the lesser of two evils to come back to 11 Creffield Road after a fortnight of my father's machinations. The kitchen always smelt of strange delicacies – burnt curries stuck to saucepans and butcher's lights smeared all over the taps and walls.

When in the Isle of Wight I always insisted on seeing Osborne House, Queen Victoria's residence. I even sat on the queen's commode when the security guard wasn't looking. My mother had started to tell me a wonderful series of adventures about a plastic doll. I called her Matilda. In design she was a cheap forerunner of the Barbie and Cindy dolls. She had red hair, nasty little plastic white heels and long thin legs. She was over the top, a parody of early Sixties or late Fifties glamour, a cartoon prostitute or a secretary trying to make it with her boss.

Matilda the Glamour Doll travelled back to Victoria's court with the aid of a magic ring. Once there she was embroiled in various plots saving the Queen from anarchists. All the Victorian worthies were involved – John Brown, Gladstone, Disraeli. There was a gallant Colonel who helped foil the plots, and escapes were made down the London sewers. Matilda, of course, only needed to rub her magic ring to wish herself back to the present.

Mum bought me my first Sherlock Holmes paperback in the Isle of Wight and I was instantly hooked. I fell in love with his dark saturnine looks and his intelligence. I am still a bit in love with him, although I realise in practical terms I would not enjoy living with a smoker and drug addict who liked to play the violin in the middle of the night. He was not a bad model to fall for though – none of the selfishness of Mr. Rochester or the violent moodiness of Heathcliff. The men I fell in love with in real life were extremely intelligent.

When it rained I stayed in and read. On fine days I played with other kids in the camp. In the first summer I had Dick as my slave. My hair was still blonde and shone in the sun. By six it had darkened irretrievably and I had gappy teeth. The little boys were less interested so I made friends and went tree climbing with a girl who had the unlikely name of Mary Christmas. By the third summer my new front teeth had come through. I was pretty again and knew it. An older boy fell for me and I ordered him to pick me winkles from some slimy rocks near the old water mill. My mother cooked the whole bucketful for me. I scoffed the lot and didn't even offer him any. The next day his mother took him home, away from my bad influence, and he left a tear-stained note pinned to my caravan door.

Summer ended and Tess had her first batch of kittens – Dapple, Hugo, Blownoutus and Hitler were the characters of the six. She gave birth to them somewhere in amongst my mother's hats and the Dr. White's towels. We decided to keep Dapple and Hugo. Hugo was the only Manx of the bunch and perfectly black. We found him a home at first, but to my relief the woman brought him back. Tess was relieved too. She was fiercely devoted to her kittens and had psychic fits in which she would wash and polish whichever cat was next to go to a home. Afterwards she would grieve for a day or two before getting on with the hard work of mothering the rest. Like most broody women she was only a good mother to babies. She often hated her progeny when they grew up to be adult cats, except for the odd favourite. She always elected a female cat to act as midwife. Dapple became that next, but she died too young to go on with the role. In a year or two both she and Hugo were wiped out by a vicious bout of cat 'flu. Tess caught it too, but recovered. For a while, her whiskers turned grey with grief and she produced a third film that she could roll right up across her eyes.

The rest of the summer passed uneventfully enough. I was thrilled at the prospect of the long holiday ahead before I went back to school. I only kept in touch with one or two friends. My favourite was Lindsay, who was from a stage family. She was hated by some of the other girls because of her prettiness. Occasionally, we'd see her disappear with her red-haired grandmother. My mother thought Lindsay was wearing make-up, lipstick at least, and we suspected she was on her way to an audition or some child modelling. Lindsay's Gran sold Avon cosmetics as a sideline to an antiques business. Her mother sang in a backing group and was divorced but friendly with her ex-husband – something my parents found slightly shocking in the days before split families were the norm.

I hoped life in the main school would be more fun. We were in a modern block beside the old building. Our form teacher, Miss Williams, was young. Although she was not as bossy on the surface as Mrs. Young was, she was in the habit of drawing senior teachers, or worse still, the Head Miss Harold's attention to the minor peccadilloes of her pupils.

I had already taught myself the rudiments of typing on my mother's portable Olivetti. I started by making up a church service, copying my father. I only got as far as a prayer or two before I gave up. I used one finger plonked down vertically on to the keys. My knuckles and wrists would ache for hours after a line or two because of the jarring motion. I did not even attempt to use my father's typewriter – a large heavy cast-iron Underwood. My father could type at demonic speed on it although he'd never been taught as my mother had. Consequently, he couldn't touch type, even though his speed far exceeded that of most people who could. He usually spoiled the look of his writing and letters by being mean with the margins.

Soon I turned to more creative forms of writing than church services. The first item I had accepted for publication was a parable. I was still only six. Why I chose this form is still a mystery to me. I still have the school magazine where it appeared in the following year.

In the desert were two merchants on mules with food. They both saw money. One rode away, but the other got off the mule to pick it up, and the mule ran away and he got left in the desert to starve.

My next effort at the age of seven was a TS Eliot parody. We had just been introduced to a few of his cat poems. My version went:

The Rum Tum Tugger was a curious cat

He shouted out bugger as he slipped upon the mat.

I did not enter that one for the magazine.

I was also becoming interested in drawing. I'd shown an early aptitude for using colour in painting. My mother had let me paint our old coalscuttle red at the age of three. Afterwards, seeing I was rather handy with a paintbrush, I was given some of her old life-drawings to colour in. I soon turned one of the female nudes into a brown monkey holding an orange. Once I turned to more analytical drawing I mainly did cats' faces or plants. Even then I was beginning to be able to draw flowers in a way that was botanically recognisable. I noticed peculiarities of colour and texture in leaves and petals. My artwork was too untidy to attract much admiration though. In later years I realised that this was a feature of every person who specialised in painting. It's only those who go into Graphics who can produce the neat pieces of colouring that teachers admire.

I also liked the effect of pencil scribbles. When you held a block of them up to the light it was like a dark mirror. You could do a piece of shading going one way and then have words within it. To my mind the effect was extremely beautiful. I was drawn to its dark subtlety. I ornamented the covers of my exercise books by shading them completely. Inside the shading were suitable logos – multiplication signs and pluses on Maths for instance. Miss Williams was horrified and would not listen to my explanation. To her the whole thing was just a nasty black mess, a wanton act of desecration. She was to be even more horrified by a later action of mine.

We had small Formica-topped light blue tables. At the end of every term we were issued a little cupful of soap powder, a brush, cloth and water to scrub them clean. During a lesson where we were meant to be writing something I finished early and idly scribbled BUM on the table in front of me. It was only in pencil. A wipe of spit or soap and water would have erased it easily enough, but Miss Williams descended on me swiftly before I could do anything. She never really told anyone off, so I didn't realise what was coming my way. The whole thing became a matter for Miss Harold instead. She was told of my infamy. My mother was summoned before her and given the name of a Harley Street psychologist to take me to. My mother suggested timidly that I might have culled the word from Shakespeare but Miss Harold had her own explanation: "They pluck these words out of the air!" She hadn't realised that I learnt that and many worse words from my refined little co-pupils.

Dr. Creek, the psychologist, cost my parents £10 in the days when that was a considerable amount of money, approximately half my father's weekly salary. Being a kindly soul, she suggested that I went on to free Child Guidance instead if the school insisted on further treatment. Unlike most poets, I can honestly say that I have been diagnosed as sane. I quite enjoyed my hour with Dr. Creek. It involved talking and playing with bricks and wooden mosaics. The bag of mosaics contained an odd number that could not be fitted into a complete pattern. What the young patient did with the extra diamond was obviously the crux of the test. Mindful of my father's ecclesiastical hobbies, or perhaps my pagan offerings to Baal, I said the extra mosaic was an altar stone laid on the mosaic floor of a church.

Child Guidance was also fun in that it gave me a legitimate excuse for one afternoon off school a week. I was given a long IQ test to start with. The examiner gave her prognosis the week after. My reading age was supposed to be twelve, which may have been an underestimation as I'd already happily consumed Paradise Lost, Dante and Hamlet. The woman went on to say: "She's backward at maths – she's only a year ahead of her age at that!" That line was symptomatic of the unfairness with which I, as a gifted child, was to be treated in the years that followed. I had to be more than slightly ahead at everything to be considered equal.

Until the age of six or seven I had wanted to be a writer and illustrator. After a few weeks of Child Guidance I began to see that being a psychologist might give me more power.

"Does Miss Harold have to listen to a psychologist?" I asked my mother. She believed that she did. That clinched it for me. Any profession that could make a headmistress jump had a certain something to be said for it.

My weekly afternoon at Child Guidance consisted of play. There were paints galore, a dolls' house, a garage with a lift, a sand-pit and lots of blocks and other bits of pieces. I almost blew my sanity verdict by building a city in the sand pit and laying rubber pipes for sewerage before pouring in rather a lot of water. As I talked enthusiastically about the sewers I saw a look of triumphant diagnosis on the analyst's face. I stopped quickly, realising I might have given too much away... After my first few visits I had sussed out the direction the psychologists were taking. At home I asked my mother for a potted history of psychology and its methods. Having studied German at university, and philosophy for one year of that course, she was reasonably well versed in the subject. She didn't quite realise why I wanted this knowledge though. Once I had learned definitions for terms like phobia and neurosis, I thought I would manufacture a comparatively harmless one to shut the psychologists up, just in case there was something really wrong. I felt a certain distaste for being analysed and for having to explain every action. I feel the same now. I believe that creative people need to keep a certain area of their brain completely private. I think of the psyche or the inner daemon as something like the air in a rubber ball. Dissect too much and all the bounce might go. I kept my bounce by manufacturing an artificial phobia to draw the psychologists' fire. One day, talking as I played, I filled the dolls' house with figures and pretended to be upset at there being lodgers in the attic. Immediately my parents were consulted. Did we have lodgers? (We didn't.) Could it be that I had become disturbed at the thought of strangers coming into the house after overhearing some family discussion? My mother thought that it could. I laughed inwardly when she reported this conversation. Soon after that it was suggested that I had no further need of therapy.

While it felt safer to be out of the psychiatrists' hands, it also meant that I lost my afternoon off school. Mum usually took me to lunch at the ABC, or for tea afterwards as a treat.

The women at Child Guidance had recommended that I be moved up a form, as I was too bright for the one I was in. That meant a bit of extra holiday work to catch up with – what the form above had learned in their first two terms. For a while, my mother said, I became duller and less fun. "Why don't you play with your dolls' house?" she said one day. "You liked playing with the one at Child Guidance." "No thanks," I replied, "You wouldn't know why I'm doing it!" It was the start of my smart-arse phase.

Chapter Ten: Uncle Terence

AT ABOUT the age of seven I started to get interested in music. I heard Joan Sutherland on the radio and suddenly wanted to be an opera singer. I had a pretty voice and could sound suitably angelic singing numbers like "Away in the Manger". Gran bought me a second-hand piano from Steers in Acton. I wanted to learn to play it straightaway. My mother wrote a note to school asking for piano lessons. There was a waiting list when we applied. Somehow things went astray and my name did not go on it. Perhaps they'd heard about the Child Guidance... It was three years before my mother agreed to chase up the matter. Her Celtic reticence and pride held her back from many things in life. When it spilled over into things that affected me, it held me back as well.

The piano was installed in *The Bull Room* as we called it. The room's name was something to do with army jargon. "Bull" as in bullshit meant an empty kind of showing off. My parents didn't tell me the whole word and I assumed that "Bull" wasn't short for anything for several years. The Bull Room had an open fire that hardly warmed it. Over the years it became fearfully cold thanks to a slipping sash window. My father pushed it up every now and again, but it was never mended. Within months, my father had lost his job and hardly any repairs were done to the house. It was a way of cutting back. When I did get a piano teacher, years later, if I practised for any length of time, my fingers would go bluish and numb with the cold. Another thing my parents saved on was a piano tuner. The instrument was untouched from when it was bought to the day it was carted off to the musical equivalent of the knacker's yard, thirty years later. It was a pretty piano, Edwardian walnut with inset mother-of-pearl. As the notes deteriorated, I had to put the soft pedal down to gain any tone. When we first had it the whole pitch was about a semitone down. It fell to slightly over a tone in the years that followed. By the time I replaced it, the whole instrument was irredeemably tuneless.

Before my mother chased up the piano lessons I had to learn a little music on my own. I used to improvise soulfully and try singing notes at the top of my range and almost the top of the piano's. If my family had had any musical know-how whatsoever, I could have been turned into a little coloratura then and there. We also enquired about singing lessons, but I was told I should wait until I was sixteen or so.

I taught myself to read music when my parents bought me a recorder. I had the rudiments of the treble clef, at any rate, in a day or so. I could also pick out any tune by ear on the piano. Some of my school friends used to come round and thump chopsticks and Mum played a few hymns. Davenport, an elderly pal of my father's, was the only good player we knew. He winced at the flatness of the piano, tried a little Bach, and then settled for teaching me to play "Trafalgar Square". You play the first four notes at the bottom, as the lions, before running a finger up the piano and plinking it on the top note for Nelson. Occasionally we also had singsongs of naval numbers like "Toll for the Brave".

I liked Davenport's musical side, but hated everything else about him. He was rich and greedy. He loved coming to stay with us. His family wealth came from textile mills in Macclesfield. He had a vintage Rolls Royce he'd park outside the door. In spite of his money, he was so unspeakably mean that he once brought my mother two stale rolls as a present after cruising on the QE2. There were occasional boxes of Black Magic too. These were saved from Christmas, and Mum only got them by the time the chocolate had acquired a grey bloom, or softened slightly.

Physically I found Davenport extremely repulsive. My mother believed that he was suffering from malnutrition because of his parsimonious diet at home. He was blind in one eye and all his hair had gone except for some baby fuzz on a pointed red pate. He was horribly long and thin and had bright red blood blisters on his lips where he had chewed them. I hated being kissed by Uncle Terence because of these blisters. To his face he was Uncle Terence, although we referred to him as Davenport, like some piece of furniture, when he was not around. Davenport's home diet consisted of one loaf of bread a week, which he'd allow to go mouldy so that he could benefit from the penicillin. He'd also buy six thin lamb chops and eat one a day. On the Lord's day he went to his sister's. Any vitamins were acquired by eating heartily elsewhere. His sister kept a generous table, as did my mother. Davenport always wanted the best and always asked for second helpings. We used to get a lavish parcel of Baxter's foods from a Miss Morrison, a Scot who lived in Australia. She had been half in love with Old Vic and wrote him

soulful letters beginning "My dear Chevalier". She continued her
generosity to my father after he died. Davenport ate a lot of the
Baxter's goodies – tinned pheasant and grouse, consommés and
peaches in brandy. I grudged him every mouthful. I suppose, looking back on it, that my parents only put up with him in the vague
expectation that some largess might come their way one day. It
never did. Those that aren't generous in life are rarely generous in
death.

Davenport was a Unitarian. My parents used to joke behind his
back that he only had one eye, one ball and one God. He was one
of a large number of closet homosexuals with religious leanings who
were drawn to my father and had similar peculiar ecclesiastical hobbies. Davenport and my father sometimes disappeared for hours
going to some strange new church. Sometimes they found one with
a bishop who'd provide a lavish tea afterwards. A West Indian leader
of a small sect treated them most kindly. They were served immense
plates of curry in an extremely hot flat in Lewisham. The central
heating was full on even in the summer. After the curry came roast
chicken, salmon, etc. The man had asked my father what his
favourite foods were beforehand, then prepared the lot. Dad was
thrilled to have an unexpected banquet and vowed to stay friendly.

A mutual friend tried to persuade them to go to another eccentric who provided feasts. The only snag was that this man was in the
habit of wearing an iron crown and demanding homage. Dad decided to give that particular bishop a miss.

Dad was also the chaplain to a number of regiments. I don't
think they quite realised how small the denominations he belonged
to were. His chaplaincies usually only involved saying Grace in BBC
accents at lavish dinners. At worst, he might have to turn out a ser-
mon on Remembrance Day. It was a task Dad loved. Fortunately no
serving officers chose to seek counselling from him on more spiri-
tual matters. My father's role of chaplain got me into a number of
regimental parties. Some of the regiments he had once served in, I
shan't say fought in. His War was exceedingly peaceful. Thanks to
flat feet he never got sent where any action was. He attained the
rank of acting Major, spending all his time teaching other men how
to fight instead. Perhaps he should have been a professional soldier.
He certainly enjoyed the life and all the bullshit. For years, before
and after the War, he mucked around playing boys' games with the

Territorials.

I looked forward to the regimental parties. One, The Kensingtons, was particularly lavish. They showed hours of cartoons and Chaplin films or a full-length Disney feature before we shovelled down jellies and got our presents from Santa. There was usually a magic display and a few games too. My father also belonged to the Institute of Journalists and I used to go to another annual party with them. This usually involved a talent contest where I was only too happy to show off and sing.

The fact that all these parties were mixed improved my behaviour. I had no wish to beat up strange little girls in front of boys I was trying to impress. At about this stage I seemed to develop two totally different images which have stayed with me ever since. I was known as a little devil and troublemaker in my school world. To others outside, I seemed more of a little angel. At every regimental or journalistic Christmas party I behaved impeccably. The woman in the local baker's too used to call me as "the politest girl in Haberdashers" after I asked her sweetly for "a fairy Hovis". If only she'd known.

At about this time my father lost his job working as a sub-editor at *The Wide World*. The new editor didn't take a shine to him and dropped hints about nepotism. He assumed that my grandfather had given him the job, not realising that Old Vic had a kind of hatred for his sons and had been slightly peeved when Dad applied for the post secretly and got it. The magazine went downhill fast as the new editor tried to modernise it. I still meet men in their sixties and seventies who loved the old-fashioned version and regret its passing. Soon *The Wide World* was no more and George Newnes was bought by IPC. There were mass redundancies in the world of journalism at this time and my father soon found himself on the scrap heap. My parents managed to keep this from me for a year or two. Dad got odd jobs as a clerk or teacher and between these lived on savings. There were all sorts of minor cutbacks. The atmosphere became more quarrelsome every time an electricity bill came in. Electricity had always been a source of family feuds. My father, being hot-blooded needed far less heating than my mother. Even before he lost his job, I was lectured on the use of lights after switching the fancy hall ones on and off a few times. "You'll bankrupt me!" my father said. I always took hyperbole literally at that age and began to imagine that there were such vast electrical surges when lights were switched on and off a few times, and that the next bill would run to hundreds. When one of the girls at my seventh birthday party switched the same lights on and off a few times, I whacked her head against the wall to save her bankrupting Dad. Deborah was taken home in tears, as were most of the other girls. I wasn't responsible for the rest. At that age girls' parties were nearer to a vicious Rugby scrum than anything else. Several girls had set on another Deborah at the same party because they envied her blue and silver nylon dress. About the only non-violent person at that party was Geeta. She sat in the corner by the piano, nervously singing nursery rhymes. My mother helped her comb and plait her long silky Indian hair while the rest of us beat each other up. When all had gone home the back bedroom looked as if a tornado had hit it. What I particularly regretted was the fact that my plastic blow-up bouncing dog had been bounced until it got a puncture and the water in the bottom that kept it upright had run into other parts of its anatomy. We blamed the daughter of an evangelistic woman who gave coffee mornings. While her daughter wasn't deeply into violence, Anne was good at a bit of quiet sturdy destruction. Anne was slightly asthmatic. My mother and father always joked about kids who were. "It's not asthma, it's ask Ma," Mum used to say. Having evolved the theory that only the children of repressive mothers got it, my mother was never able to acknowledge my condition when I developed it a few years later. I had several attacks in my teens, but had to find ways of coping. If she'd ever called the doctor, she'd have had to acknowledge that she was one of the repressive mothers she'd joked about, or else that her theory was all wrong. Somehow she couldn't bring herself to do either...

Chapter Eleven: Back to Nature

IN THE SUMMER term I joined Miss Young's form and found, for the first time, a teacher who liked me. The only problem was that she was a little hard of hearing and did not always hear my replies. Eventually she told my mother that I was deaf and should be examined by the doctor.

We went to Dr. Mason's one evening. My mother liked him because he was very refined and Scottish. He spent most weekends in Edinburgh, flying back to Heathrow on the Monday morning. It was a short enough journey to allow him to get to work early. His house and surgery were full of good antiques. His wife's paintings hung on the walls. She had exhibited at the Paris Salon, he boasted. He looked absolutely ancient to me, pretty much of an age with the antiques. He shook slightly as he examined my ears. There was, of course, absolutely nothing wrong with them. From that day to this, I've found that people always see their own faults in me. Miss Young had to accept the doctor's verdict, just as Miss Harold, more reluctantly, had to cope with the fact that a sane kid might enjoy words like bum.

The rest of the term passed uneventfully enough. Looking back at those times, my mother believes that I got a little boring after my treatment, almost normal in fact. At school, some of the work seemed almost unbearably easy, spelling lessons in particular. We had to make up sentences using words it was considered we might have difficulty with. To amuse myself, I sometimes did this in the shape of poems. One of my efforts went:

On the floor was the flour,
The milk was quite sour,
Undrunk was the stout,
The fire had gone out.

My mother was slightly worried when she read that one. Would the teachers think our place was like that? "Sounds like an Irish slum!" she said. Coming from South Wales she had grave doubts about the Irish. In that part of the country, for decades, they had been immigrant workers prepared to do dirty dangerous jobs for poor wages. The Welsh who had aspirations liked to disassociate themselves. Yet, my mother probably had a little dash of the Hibernian herself. Her maiden name was Banfield, often an Irish name, and her grandfather came from Glasgow...

Though I seemed to be learning nothing I didn't know already in lessons, there were tricks I picked up in the playground from other girls. I learned to stretch a piece of grass taut between my thumbs and blow through it till it vibrated with a high whistling sound. Sometimes we also made our hands into an instrument, blowing in that same space between the thumbs with our hands cupped behind. By slowly moving the fingers away one could make higher notes. With large long-fingered hands like mine a full scale was possible. It was an age when we liked to make tools of our hands and bodies. We all started to play cats' cradle with string round our fingers and we had a game which involved a longer string made of dozens of rubber bands which went round the feet of two girls who jumped their way into different criss-cross patterns. I wanted, also, to learn hopscotch. I'd read about it in Victorian novels. But the game had died out, it seemed. Though most people had heard of it, I couldn't find anyone who knew the rules.

I made a new set of friends in my class. The old friendships broke up almost instantaneously; they had only been based on proximity. I got on particularly well with Jennifer Mark. Her parents, like mine, were not rich. There was a slight exoticism about her background. Her mother came from India. Although Jennifer was mainly Scottish and boasted descent from Robert Burns, the other girls speculated that she might have a bit of Indian or Parsee blood, a possibility which sounded interesting. When I visited her house for tea her mother talked of the exotic fruits she'd grown up eating. I particularly liked the sound of "custard apples". I have never managed to taste one yet.

Tess was on to her second litter of kittens by now and I was proud to show them off to my new found friends. We kept two out of that litter. One of them was a dappled black and white with a perfect, slightly stout, Manx shape and a little stump instead of a tail. I called him John Bunyan. When I saw him as a new kitten with closed eyes and a smile on his purring face, he reminded me of the author of The *Pilgrim's Progress* whose usual portrait is of a man caught dreaming. The other was also a Manx, but odder-looking. Professor Moriarty was mostly black with a white bib and nose. He was very long with a sharp pointed behind. When stroking him in the dark it was easy to mistake this for his neck and end up with your hands on his arse. Being a kinky and slightly malevolent cat, he enjoyed catching us unaware.

Bunyan and Morry were as different as chalk and cheese. Bunyan was his mother's favourite and always got the best teat. He was very good-tempered as a kitten but became less so as a fat adult, always over-hot under his thick coat. Morry was loathed on sight by his mother. If she could shake him off or cover the worst and lowest teat with a leg so that he couldn't get it, she would do so. A few years later he was to infect her with influenza. He'd caught it because she'd hounded him out in appalling weather. She died and he survived. Perhaps Tess sensed that he'd be the end of her one day.

I loved both Morry and Bunyan passionately. Bunyan was like a great cuddly bunny, but thick as pig-shit. He once sat on a warm apple pie by mistake for a cushion. Morry by contrast was clever. He had to find ways of surviving after his mother's rejection. He was weaned and foraging on his own at three weeks. Before reaching adult-size, he was already twisting doorknobs to get out and putting electric lights on. His extreme length and thinness made him more agile than most cats. He enjoyed putting the light on over my parents' bed, whenever he had lured one of them to stroke his headless neck at the nether end. He'd bash the switch on a cord against the wall till the light came on so that he could see the reactions after they shouted "Urgh!"

When Bunyan and Morry were old enough, Dad took them to Dr. Benjamin in Paddington for castration. Bunyan was already highly sexed with incestuous leanings. He had already tried it on with both his mother and brother. Any orifice would do. I understood about the process of giving birth, but had not given much thought to how creatures got pregnant in the first place. When I saw Bunyan on his Mum or trying it on with Morry, I assumed the cats were giving each other piggybacks.

Unfortunately Dad made the mistake of letting both brothers travel in the same box to the vet. When they came to after the operation, each believed the other was responsible. Terrible howls of rage erupted from the basket on the way home and long furry arms poked out through the wicker window. From then on it was all out war. Bunyan almost blinded Morry and he tore a large strip of fur off his brother's lower belly in revenge. If Bunyan had not already been castrated, Morry would certainly have done it for him. It was decided that the two cats could never be allowed to inhabit the same room together again. Dad put Morry in the chapel for sanctuary. Within a few weeks he had desecrated the place thoroughly. He kicked the crosses into his food and urinated on the altar. "It was like a Black Mass!" Mum said when Dad allowed her in to clean up.

There were no cat doors so Dad operated a kind of shift system whereby Morry had certain hours of freedom. The only problem was that Morry was devoted to Dad and would not bother to return to the house for anyone else. When Mum failed to get him back and into sanctuary so that other cats could go out, Dad would snarl with impatience and go out to demonstrate how easy it all was. Then, we'd see him walking up the garden with a cat on his shoulders. Morry would ride upstairs like that, with all his hair bristling if he passed his mother or brother on the way. Morry would roam the house in the evening while the others were shut into the kitchen for the night. Often he sat on the landing inspecting and licking his minute pink dick. I called it his "Chinese checker". It looked remarkably like the small plastic ones in my pocket set.

Morry lived on to over sixteen and became a gentle kind soul in old age. Only a few years after he started living in the chapel, the whole area was converted to North Sea gas. The men from the Gas Board came to check all the appliances first. Dad decided not to allow them into the chapel. "The fire's the same as that in the front attic," he said. "Besides, I've got an elderly sick black gentlemen in there. He doesn't want to be disturbed." The gasmen were very understanding.

Some cats are quietly filthy, others do it all in public. Morry was unusual; he did both. As if the desecration of the chapel wasn't enough, he urinated in a huge antique clock of the sort that once hung in shops. It had been lying on the floor prior to being mounted on the wall. Once one cat has pissed on an object, others feel they have to compete. Bunyan and Morry took turns in personalising it. Morry also had his wicked way all over the cellar. He'd pad down there of an evening and roll in the coal dust. Sometimes his bib turned black with it. Years later we discovered several dozen well-hidden turds that had gone mouldy and grown fur with age. They looked like small animals, so we christened them Morrypoms. They were sold with the house.

In spite of Morry's bad habits he was a modest soul. His sensibilities were so developed that he had the capacity to blush. I've only known one other cat who could do this. I loved to exploit his weakness. If he was sitting by the fire in the evening I'd remove my navy school knickers and lift my skirt and say: "Look Morry, here's my fanny!" I don't know whether it was the word or the sight, but Morry would always hang his head and his white nose would turn extremely pink.

Apart from flashing at the cat, I went on developing my botanical knowledge. I was using a section of the garden at home as a weed sanctuary. Some plants made their own way there naturally. Others were taken from wasteland. Occasionally I put in requests to relative for specific items like a jack-in-the-pulpit. My aunt, Dorothy, had to bring a specimen with her when she visited from Wales. It was planted in the back garden and flourished there. (Curiously, when I moved to St. Leonards, although I did not take the plant, another appeared to welcome me by the front gate in an otherwise empty flowerbed.) There was a surprisingly rich choice of weeds in Ealing. There was very little on the commons, but plenty between the pavement stones and on a rough bit of land used for parking in the unmade-up Daniel Road. Here, I was stunned by the exotic beauty of a huge poisonous thorn apple, a wild fig tree, a tangle of hops and a delicate pale blue milk vetch. The land around the building used for my preparatory school had been rich in different grasses like Yorkshire Mist and wild barley. We used to break off the heads of the latter and drop them down each other's sleeves or stick them on our school jumpers. We did this with small sticky burdock burs too. We only went to our sports field once a week, but there was another bit of land we were allowed to play on next to the primary school. Eventually a new gym was built on it, but while it was just a field, I learned to make daisy chains there and we experimented using the acrid juice of greater celandine to burn our hands. Mine seemed unharmed by it, as my skin seems to have a good tolerance to many plant poisons.

My love of natural history was to be given more shape by my next teacher, Miss Davies. She pleased my mother by calling me "a regular little professor". I was not a favourite because she was too fair to treat any child in that way, but she did suggest titles of nature books for me, and societies I could join. She had a plain but likeable face with a freckled skin that reminded me of oatmeal. She always wore sensible tweeds and flat shoes and went bird watching at week-ends. She suggested to my mother that I go to Kew. I did and got hooked. A couple of years later, once I had a bike, I used to cycle over and spend a chunk of most Saturdays there. Miss Davies hoped her enthusiasm would rub off on all the class, but most were city kids, completely uninterested in country life. They sniggered behind her back when she had parcels of birds' wings sent for us to examine. The feathers were beautiful but the wings got slightly high in a centrally heated classroom.

We had a school trip to a farm where we helped harvest the potatoes and ran around looking at various plants. I roamed happi-ly, loving the beautiful spindleberries in the woodland. A half-Italian girl, Andrea, was enraged by my easy identification of every-thing and snarled "Mrs. Clever" as I filled in my list and question-naire. Nearer to Haberdashers' we were taken for a half-day in Perivale Wildlife Sanctuary. I returned to the Sanctuary a week later with my father and, although we weren't members, we managed to bluff our way into borrowing the key so that I could have another look. Dad also took me on outings to Epping and Hainault. He loved collecting places although he didn't care a toss about nature. Hainault and Epping were tube stations at the end of the Central line. Every station was a place to be visited. But, he'd have much preferred simply to put one of his flat feet out of the train on to the platform, then hop back on. Walking was never a joy to him. He'd applied the foot over the boundary, or off the train, technique to many places in Britain. There were times when he took me to points where I could stand with a leg in each of two counties. He loved statistics more than the experience of life. He was an avid reader of guidebooks and had sent away for brochures of every town in Britain. Most of his investments too were small amounts of money loaned to different town councils.

My best source for unusual weeds proved to be Chorley Wood in Bucks. Dad had been born in Amersham and liked to revisit places near his old home. Chorley Wood was a paradise for the col-lection of wild flowers and fungi. Several types of land were mixed together within a mile or two – woodland, meadow and marsh pro-viding a vast variety of different plants. Years later much of the land was taken for road building and we ceased to visit. Miss Davies kept a nature table and I brought in weeds from time to time. An autumn visit to Chorley Wood yielded a wonderful crop of toadstools: Beefsteak Fungus, Tawny Grisettes, Dryad's Saddle, and Shaggy Ink-Cap. Miss Davies had recommended a good book on the subject. She was so old-fashioned that she was slightly shocked at the extravagance when my mother went out and bought it for me rather than waiting till my birthday. I identified all my specimens with the book's help. Then I made my first mistake. Flowers kept fresh in water, so I figured the same would work for toadstools. They all went in the upstairs bath. My parents were ordered to use only the downstairs one until Monday. Needless to say all my fungi turned into a slimy mess and never found their way to the nature table. At that stage I had not thought of eating them, I was to turn to that only in Hastings, many years later.

Part of my liking for fungi stemmed from the images conjured by their strange names. I was also particularly fond of flowers that sounded as if they might have a peculiar history behind them: Dame's violet, Bridget-in-her-bravery, Star of Bethlehem. In the Victorian period, a man from my father's family, Pycraft (Christian name William, perhaps) had been a botanist. Mum swore she saw one of his books in the Isle of Wight, but her holiday money had run out. I have never been able to track any of his botany books down since, even in the British library catalogue, although there are a few bird books by a William Plane Pycraft who may be the same person. Pycraft is a rare name that comes from Yarmouth. My father's grandmother Lydia came from a seafaring family. I am supposed to look a bit like her. She enjoyed jellied eels, stout and young men and lay around naked at eighty to show off a body that was still in pretty good nick. I heard this rare surname again recently when the Telegraph asked me about a bad buy. I nominated an amaryllis I had bought which did not flower. Lo and behold, a David Pycraft was brought in as a gardening expert to comment. I wondered if he was a distant cousin descended from that botanist.

I tried desperately to please Miss Davies. I recorded the birds that visited my garden, but she mostly disbelieved me. Yet Ealing was rich in birds that came for the gardens of flowering trees and the commons full of horse chestnuts. Wasn't it conceivable that a bullfinch might have come across the two or three miles from Perivale Sanctuary or that a raven might have made a day-trip up river from the Tower? Miss Davies was beginning to believe I was a

liar, although that's never been one of my faults. The last straw was
when I saw a wallaby on a lead, taken by its owner to the Lyric
Theatre in Hammersmith. Needless to say the wallaby had not been
house-trained and had a slight accident on the red carpet in the
foyer. I told Miss Davies and was greeted with utter disbelief. It's
impossible to tell now whether I misidentified the bullfinch and the
raven, but I am absolutely sure about the wallaby. There was a
whole theatre crowd there to witness the sight. If Miss Davies did-
n't believe what I had seen in my back garden or in the theatre at
Christmas time, then I would have to bring her real life specimens.
One weekend my father's help was solicited to carry a seven-foot
sample of giant hogweed from a weedy patch under a bridge somewhere between West Ealing and Southall. We took it back with us
on the 207 bus. The conductor didn't bat an eyelid. Neither my
father nor myself suffered any harm from the plant. Years later, I
was to discover that it brought out rashes on some people by ren-
dering them more sun-sensitive. My latest specimen was stood in a
bucket in the corner of the classroom by itself, a fit emblem of the
show-off pest who'd brought it.

Chapter Twelve: A Cold Winter

THAT WINTER WAS freezing cold with about a foot of snow. I loved
it, but Mum had always been paranoiacally afraid of falling down on
ice. My father or I had to get all the shopping in. The only time she
ventured out in the snow was a trip to the end of the garden to cas-
trate my snowman. I had made a wonderful six-foot high one. I
reached the top of it by standing on a little step or two of snow I'd
made at its foot. I gave him cinders for eyes and a dirty grin. About
half way down I smeared more cinders for pubic hair and pinched
one of Mum's carrots for a penis. Mum's sense of bourgeois propri-
ety proved even greater than the snow-phobia and she trudged
down the garden to emasculate my creation. Neither my father nor
I would oblige. It was his kind of joke. He and the other men were
continually fooling round with penis-like objects in his army days.
One of them clutched a little speckled fungus to his flies and asked
the others: "Do you think I should see the MO?" It made my father
so happy he was still talking about it twenty years later.

While marooned inside in the cold weather, my mother and I
made a game that was a collection of faces that were sectioned in
three divisions. If you measured across and put the nose in the same
area and always made the face width the same, the sections were all
interchangeable. A pirate's headgear could go on Queen Elizabeth's
nose and Henry the Eighth's double chins and broad shoulders.
Mum was a tolerable watercolourist and her versions were much
better than mine were. She was particularly proud of her Henry the
Eighth. I sometimes cheated and made grotesque monsters out of
two chins joined, or faces with four eyes and no nose.

The snow was beginning to melt in February when we went
down to Mumbles for a few days. Gran had been ill for some
months. My mother's younger sister and her family had lived with
her for some time. Auntie Dor was doing most of the nursing, waiting on her hand and foot. Everyone but Gran knew that she had
cancer of the oesophagus. In the days before microsurgery, this was
definitely inoperable. Even now, it's not the easiest form of cancer
to treat. Gran was sent home from hospital. She had only stayed
there for a few days for tests. My grandfather had a horror of illness
and had visited her only once. "I hate hospitals!" he said to excuse
himself. A year later, by some awful quirk of fate, a woman's ward

was changed to a man's ward, and he died in the very same bed.

Back at home in Mumbles, Dorothy and my grandfather had to watch Gran getting thinner and thinner. She never complained of any pain. Perhaps she didn't feel any. She tried the morphia that the doctor left, but didn't like the sensations it gave her. She preferred to face her illness in full possession of her faculties.

I had just about stopped believing in Father Christmas, but I still believed in miracles. I thought a few prayers from myself plus muttering a few rituals while dancing widdershins round the garden might just do the trick. While I was sorry to see my beloved Gran ill, I assumed it would all come right pretty soon. I went on one or two trips with my cousins while Mum helped with the nursing. She had brought a few delicacies that Gran might be able to swallow – Brand's chicken essence, muesli, Baxter's soups, grape juice and Lucozade. Gran tried valiantly, but the results were much the same.

Mum left a sodden pile of pink Kleenex by her mother's bed. Strangely Gran couldn't associate this with her illness. She said to the others: "Olive seems very depressed about something. She's always crying. Try and cheer her up."

The snow had melted and spring was in the air. We walked along the cliffs at Langland and I found the first violets of the year. When I went back to Haberdashers' the following week, I wrote excitedly about this, rather than Gran's illness.

A month later, Gran was critically ill and close to death. We returned to Mumbles for the final stage. I was sent to Swansea Market with money to buy flowers. I chose white chrysanthemums, her favourite. When I came back, I was told Gran was too ill to see me. I insisted after a while and took my flowers in. She was a little better then, so I had a few last words with her. By the morning she was dead.

My mother had known death was imminent. One morning Gran said: "Somebody died here last night? Was it you?" Then she felt my mother's plump arms and said: "No, it must have been me. There were three of us went through the door and only one came back. It was good there." My mother tried to hide her tears. The room felt full of happiness. Gran was smiling and lit up. The small electric fire was on and the whole place seemed full of some kind of radiance and warmth. Mum believed then that Gran would die that night. Yet, Gran seemed much better and slept through without once being sick. She died the day after, two days after her dream.

My grandfather, who believed that men should not cry under any circumstances, shook his head and said: "But Dr. Porter told me she was very strong!" Gran had last been seen by that doctor when giving birth to one of her children who were all now middle-aged.

Mum believed that you should view the dead, however young you were. Without that sight, she believed that you would always believe they were still alive. I went in to look at Gran alone. She looked thin and beautiful in death with her emaciated body covered and just the face showing. Her rosy skin had refined and become porcelain-pale on a liquid diet and she had lost several stone in weight. I didn't know then that she was half-German and had been christened Ernestine Wilhelmine, a name which she later changed to Cissie. I was not told that she was the illegitimate daughter of a Bristol girl, Harriet Richardson, and a German poet until two years later. In her coffin, my mother felt, Gran looked like an Austrian aristocrat rather than the old Welsh woman everyone else believed her to be.

We all sat around weeping that night. I watched half-admiringly as my cousin Angela cried out melodramatically: "God, why didn't you take me instead!" I recognised the emotion up to a point, but still saw the logic of God (or Fate) in making this decision. Gran was seventy-two and Angela was only a teenager with a life ahead to live. Soon after Angela's mood changed to malevolence when she thought that the musical jug from the front room was to go to another relative. She managed to keep the jug.

Within a few days there was a huge funeral. While Mum believed I should see the corpse, she didn't trust me for a public solemn occasion. I was to go to friends of the family with my cousin Linda. My grandfather took over a lot of the arranging of the funeral. He was in his element arranging services. "Abide with me" and "Guide me O thou Great Jehovah" which was written by his ancestor, William Williams of Pantycelyn, were the chief hymns to be sung. A huge turnout was expected. Gran had been very popular. Apart from the local members of the Plymouth Brethren and distant relatives, Gran had regularly given Woodbines to old men at the local workhouse. There was the possibility that everyone she had ever been kind to might turn up. They did.

In Wales, a funeral is not only a solemn occasion, it is also an excuse to invade a neighbour's house and inspect it from top to bottom for badly-done chores and dust lurking under beds and ornaments. Those whose houses don't come up to scratch are generally reckoned to have English blood. Auntie Dor, my other Aunt, Kathleen, and Mum got a massive cleaning operation underway to avoid any such slur. Day by day, friends and relatives dropped in to pay their respects, leave flowers, be entertained and look for dust.

I was shuffled round to various relatives labelled Aunt or Uncle. Most of them were not my aunts or uncles, but aunts or uncles of cousins or my mother. Luckily I was in my charming mode. I talked gardening with "Uncle George" and played unhygienic games with my mother's cousin Magdalene's children. They had opened a "shop" on some shelves, full of unwashed used Kitekat tins. It was a miracle we managed not to cut ourselves on the ragged tin lids.

In the evenings I was introduced to other distant cousins. For the first time for many years my mother met her third cousin, Elwyn. He was a six foot four ex-miner and still handsome. He was a clever man but had opted for the mines rather than leaving his part of Wales. Mum had fancied both him and his brother Gareth when they were children together. But a better job called her away to England. From then on she would only return to Wales as an outsider.

By this stage, my more malevolent persona was beginning to creep out, so I turned somersaults on the sofa while Mum tried to talk to her long-lost cousins. Elwyn turned round and said: "What's the matter *bach*?" *Bach*, meaning little, is an endearment in Welsh. All my mother's second cousins were Welsh-speakers. Her own immediate family hadn't been.

I became charming again now I had a bit of notice. It's often all a naughty kid needs. The Welsh recognise that, as do Italians and most other child-loving nations. The English do not.

On the actual day of the funeral, I was sent with my cousin Linda to her godmother, Mrs. Taylor. I was in angelic mode and she was impressed as I won a quiz on Biblical knowledge hands down over my Methodist cousins. Some members of the family assumed I would be ignorant of all things religious as my mother had left the sect and moved to England. At teatime I went with Linda to her grandparents, the Jewells. They had been to the funeral but left from the graveyard in order to give us a huge Welsh tea. I managed to clear enough shepherd's pie to feed a shepherd and his dog for a week. After that, the first disaster of the day, I got stuck in their upstairs lavatory when the handle came loose. (No, the shepherd's pie hadn't had dire results.) I kept calm and Linda's granddad, Edgar, talked through the door as the offending handle was removed and the door prised open.

When I arrived back in Mumbles, all the washing up was stacked on the side to dry. Mum and Auntie Dor had just served tea and ham sandwiches to sixty people who had come to "pay their respects". There had been at least twice that number in the chapel earlier in the day and others at the graveyard. Gran had been given a good send-off. I had seen various relatives and helpers making sandwiches at breakfast. They had been spreading and cutting for hours. There were still a few left and naturally I sampled them. I've never been one for limiting myself to three meals a day.

Within a day or two we returned home. There was a small redistribution of Gran's things. Mum got back some of the recent gifts she'd given her mother, including a gold lustre teapot, which was eventually stolen from us.

In school again on the Monday I had to write up what I'd done at the weekend. I just sat and left my page blank. It would have seemed like an act of trivialisation to write one of our few line essays: "Went to Mumbles for a few days. Gran died and there was a funeral and I met lots of new relatives." Instead I wrote nothing. When the student teacher came round and asked me why I sat silently. I was afraid I'd break down if I put it into words. I felt I had a right to my silence and the blank page before me at that moment in time. Fortunately the bell went before the teacher could press me further. Pretty soon life went on as normal although, for the future, there would be less trips to Wales.

Chapter Thirteen: Hate at First Sight

THE FOLLOWING AUTUMN I entered Miss Brook's class. I had already been the victim of one act of sadism by her and eventually would receive much more. While I was in Miss Davies's form she had pretended a certain interest in me and offered the chance of joining her class' visit to *Toad of Toad Hall*. I was thrilled at the prospect. One day she was supervising the dinners and she caught me leaving the onions off my hamburger behind on the plate. School onions were limp slices that had been left lying in gravy all the morning. Few but the most dedicated onion-lovers could manage to eat them.

Miss Brook promptly filled my melamine platter with all of the onions that had been left behind in the great metal dish that the cooks served from. I was ordered to eat the lot, If I did not, I could kiss goodbye to the trip to the theatre, I was told.

I was in a quandary. I knew for certain that I would be sick or have diarrhoea if I ate that quantity of onions. On the other hand, I did desperately want to see *Toad of Toad Hall*... I did the best I could and pretended to eat, chomping away visibly with a contented smile on my face, then shovelling the onions into the pocket of my overall, every time Miss Brook averted her gaze. I put my hand up afterwards and asked "May I be excused?" – the standard Haberdashers' euphemism for needing a trip to the lavatory. I quickly emptied my pocket down the pan and returned with the problem solved and my theatre visit to look forward to. "There, that wasn't so bad, was it?" Miss Brook said and I was able to say "No," quite truthfully. My mother thoroughly approved when I told her the story, even though she had a smelly overall to wash. She liked it when I beat the system quietly though she was averse to any public standing out against it.

I made friends that term with a girl, Lucinda, who had been left down from the previous one. We were the best in the class at mental arithmetic; Lucinda would usually come top with a mark or two more than me. We also both had a streak of the comic and were not appreciated by teachers. Lucinda was plump which made her something of an outsider. Again, I found myself picking friends from this category. My friends at this time also included Angela Goto who was half-Japanese and Felicity who was Irish. Again there were slight eccentricities that took my fancy. Angela was to lose most of these as time went on, but Felicity kept them. Angela and I, at this stage, loved to hang upside down from bus-shelters like a couple of monkeys or do headstands on the sofas in each other's houses. Angela's first few years had been spent in Burma and she swam much better than the rest of us after years of practice in a warm sea. I was slightly jealous of this ability.

Felicity was initially Jennifer Mark's friend. They went riding together. I'd have liked to go too, but my parents believed it was too expensive. They liked Felicity though and we had tea in each other's houses. One day, my mother was out in the front garden pruning the hydrangeas when she looked in to see myself and several other girls comparing our bare bottoms close to the piano in the front room window. She laughed to herself and hoped the neighbours hadn't seen.

Felicity lived in a bungalow in Osterley with a wonderful rambling garden about an acre in size. One of the walls of the garden abutted Osterley Manor. I jumped down about six foot from this wall and a ladder had to be lowered for my return. There were all sorts of adventures to be had in Felicity's garden. It had a small well and various outhouses. In one of these Felicity offered us a cup of "coffee" from a Billycan. Suspicious of the fact that the can was cold, I was the only child sensible enough not to sip her mud cocktail.

At tea, afterwards, there were lots of prawns. We were largely unappreciative of this delicacy because we'd heard tales that they screamed when inserted in a glass of water and we were also squeamish about their eggs. We thought they might hatch inside us. While we graduated to the cake, leaving most of the shellfish uneaten, Felicity asked her mother: "What does bugger mean? Fiona taught me the word."

Lucinda was a champion swearer and taught me her latest acquisitions. I ran home and told my mother I'd heard a new word: "Fluck!" Lucinda soon learnt better and corrected it. From her I acquired the colourful phrases: "Fuck a duck" and "Shit a brick". She claimed her father exclaimed the latter when the Bishop of Kensington refused to ordain him.

Miss Brook had more of a penchant for geography than natural history, so our next school trip was to the rather boring Commonwealth Institute. We started having to draw little maps and

learn the exports of various countries we'd never been to. Miss
Brook also had a certain liking for English and Drama. She was
friendly with the Speech teacher Miss Judd. Miss Judd gave lessons
after school as well as her weekly class. It was hinted that my Welsh
accent should be straightened out. Miss Judd had certain obvious
favourites. She adored Shona who was our smug form captain. In
our first attempt at a school play, Shona was instantly cast without
auditions as the princess, a fact that pissed all the rest of the class
off. About half a dozen of us, including myself, were her ladies-in-
waiting. We were given a line or two to say, all of which pertained
to telling her how beautiful she was. It was a remarkably ill chosen
piece for twenty spiteful nine or ten year old kids. It wasn't long
before I plotted to rewrite the play's lines. When Shona asked us
how she looked we were to reply in turn: "Disgusting!" "Ghastly!"
"Ugly as sin!" etc. The play was only being performed in class and
there was no audience except the rest of the girls. When the next
lesson came round and Shona said her lines, I bobbed a mocking
curtsy and shouted "Disgusting!" with feeling. Then Angela who
came next, meekly faltered: "Beautiful!" I realised I was betrayed.
Miss Judd was livid and I was given a good ticking-off.

In the beginning of the Spring Term something happened that
was to scar me mentally and fix my views about law and punishment
forever. I was suspected of and punished for a mean act I had not
committed. To this day, if I were asked to serve on a jury, I know
that I could not find anyone guilty, because I believe in the possibility of smoke without fire and human injustice. For the same reason I could never back anything irreversible like the death penalty.
If I had been on trial for murder in a country where that operated
and Miss Brook had been my judge I'd have been dead meat. Most
of my other opinions have shifted. I've tried Christianity, Pagan
polytheism, Atheism. At times I've had faith in magic, at others I've
believed everything is down to the individual. With all my shifting
philosophies that one belief has remained constant in my head since
I was nine. I know in my guts more clearly than I know anything
else that an accused person might be innocent and that all irreversible punishments are therefore the ultimate crime, the ultimate
blasphemy. That is the one belief that I am absolutely sure I will
never change. I have Miss Brook to thank for that. It was a lesson
worth learning, but it was a very painful one.

Haberdashers' was very good at getting us all to make useless articles. I hate to think how many hours we spent on these futile feminine pursuits. We had already made binca covers with Holy Bible embroidered on them, and now for our "Handwork" lesson we were busily stitching canvas place mats with brightly coloured raffia. One day a crowd of us gathered at lunchtime to see something that had been pushed down one of the lavatories. It turned out to be Ruth Flavin's "Handwork". Miss Brook dispersed us all to the classroom. The culprit, she decided, had to be someone who'd asked to be "excused" that morning. Little bladders not being very capacious, that meant about half of us could have been under suspicion. Curiously, she could only remember me. Then followed weeks and weeks of accusations and questionings. She was determined I'd done the dirty deed and that she was going to make me confess, whatever it took. Ruth had got a higher mark for art that week and Miss Brook assumed I was jealous. Many years later, I discovered who had really done it, long after I left school. The motive had been jealousy, but it was completely unconnected to art. Ruth was a natural athlete and a friend of hers, another athletic girl who usually came second to her in races, had dumped her handwork down the loo. Sports can be very unsporting but teachers rarely suspect them.

Miss Brook carried on a systematic campaign against me for weeks. She would come into class when someone else was teaching me and take me out for questioning. Then I was repeatedly ordered to confess until I broke down and cried. Then I'd be ordered not to be silly and to clean myself up and go back in. Afterwards, I was of course in no fit state to learn anything. I reported all this to my parents but they would do nothing. My mother was fearful I'd be expelled if she rocked the boat.

I became so unhappy that I began to wonder if suicide by toadstool might not be a good idea. But part of me wanted to turn the situation around. I managed to persuade Ruth Flavin, at any rate, that I was not guilty. My immediate friends believed me too. I enrolled them all in something called "The Just Club". We were all into starting clubs then. Girl by girl, I began to persuade the rest of the class I was innocent.

Miss Brook disbanded the club as soon as she found out about it. Her final trick was to tell the whole class that they'd be kept in if I did not confess there and then. I still had the courage to hold on, although I do not suppose it made me very popular. We weren't kept long when her bluff was called. She had no excuse for what she was doing. It wouldn't pay for all the parents to find out.

I felt no animosity whatsoever to the girl who let me bear Miss Brook's persecution. Seeing what that teacher put me through, seeing my daily fits of tears, how could she dare own up? For years I bore Miss Brook animosity though. As I began to become famous as a writer I fantasised about being on *This is Your Life*. She would appear from my past and I'd tell her publicly what I thought of her. That will never happen of course. Recently, I received a note from the Old Girls' Association saying that she had died and asking if I would like to contribute to a memorial for her. It was only then that I found out she was called Monica.

Miss Brook's persecution petered out eventually by the end of the spring term. Being a gossip she had told every other teacher in the building of my 'crime'. Miss Judd reproved me obliquely for it when I drew a caricature of her. (The caricature was horribly like her. That was the trouble.) However hard I tried in class, I could do nothing right. Miss Brook had begun to find fault with every essay I wrote. She would set bizarrely silly subjects like "A Day in the Life of a Traffic Light" then label me as facetious if I made any jokes. My traffic light engineered the crash of a load from an off licence and winked at pretty girls. I ended the essay saying: "He was fond of women and wine." I'd picked this phrase up from my father who'd used it about his latest employer. The concept was thought extremely wicked and I found myself sent to Miss Harold to be reproved for my bad behaviour. I had to take a pile of my class work. I arranged this carefully and intelligently. The essay on autumn that I knew was excellent by any standard was placed second. Some fairly good stuff was on the top and the bottom and the bad hidden in the middle, including my randy boozy traffic light story.

Miss Harold did her usual pompous best to make me feel small and as usual did not succeed. I saw her as easily manipulated and predictable, just as I had begun to see the psychoanalysts in that way. Another year of a different kind of unpleasantness from another teacher was to complete the process of alienation, I was to lose all faith in authority and all will to succeed in school terms. I was to become a lazy cheat, offloading all the work I could on to the mother who had not stood up for my rights and who had allowed me to be bullied sadistically by a sick teacher.

I had been brought up a Christian and believed the words in the New Testament which said that God would give you anything you asked in his Son's name. I prayed and prayed that my name would be cleared and Miss Brook would declare my innocence to the class, but nothing happened. My parents and God were deaf to my entreaties. The only progress I had made was through my own tiny efforts to clear my name, speaking to Ruth and the other girls one by one. For the time I gave up my faith in everything human and divine.

Just what were Miss Brook's motives? Years before, she had singled me out and praised me to my mother. In any room she noticed me first and exhibited a sort of strange love-hate attraction. I did not understand this then. Although she married eventually, I believe she was a lesbian with strong sadomasochistic tendencies. In some way she was forcing a response and a reaction of an emotional kind from a child she was drawn to. What she did to me was as much child abuse as any more direct action.

Chapter Fourteen: My First Dildo

AFTER MISS BROOK I went to Miss Overton's class. It was the first time our year was split into two. A few new girls had joined. Miss Nelson, a Scripture teacher, took one form; I was in the other. Most of my friends, except Angela, had ended up in the other class. The third forms were in the main school on the garden side. On the first day we were all asked where we'd been on holiday. Most girls had been abroad, mainly Spain or France. Angela's family regularly went to Brittany.

Miss Overton had studied at the Sorbonne and loved all things French. Anything English was second best and anything Celtic was positively disgusting. I volunteered the information that I'd been to Mumbles. The sound of the word made most of the girls snigger. It is a pretty strange name for a place.

"Where on earth's that?" Miss Overton snapped. "Wales," I faltered. "It's on the Gower peninsula."

"You went to Wales!" she said with the utmost contempt. "I should have thought you might have gone somewhere more interesting!" Did she really believe that a child who is less than ten years old has any choice in the matter? I knew from the moment I heard the contempt in her voice that I was not in for a good time. While Miss Overton was not a disturbed cruel woman like Miss Brook, she was a culture snob. From then on I was to come up against constant snubs and snide remarks. It's curious, while racial prejudice against those of a different colour is now thought unacceptable amongst educated people, the prejudice of Saxon against Celt is still prevalent and still openly voiced.

Shortly after joining Miss Overton's form we had to sit the "Eleven-plus", which was in my case, the Ten-minus. Fortunately I passed easily and my parents knew that I would have free schooling for the rest of my time in Haberdashers'. An IQ style of test was one that I liked. Like mental arithmetic, I knew that a teacher couldn't pretend I'd failed simply because she didn't like me. There was a right answer and a wrong answer. It was as simple as that. By the end of Miss Overton's form, I had begun to hate English. I tried hard at first and wrote her colourful essays. I still have copies of them and they were outstanding for a child of ten. Yet, Miss Overton, with her prejudice against the poor kid with a Welsh accent who didn't go anywhere "interesting" for her holiday was determined to give me poor or grudging marks. "Her work's not all that good, you know," she said to my mother at the parents' meeting that term.

Several of the girls in my class had also begun to take exception to my Welsh accent and make fun of it. I had given up Miss Judd's extra Speech classes when she sided with Miss Brook against me. Although I enjoyed drama and reciting poems, I was never to return to them. I was to keep my Welsh accent, it seemed. I still have it now, although, living in the South of England has modified my vowels. Yet, there are still odd words in which it is apparent, not so much to the Welsh themselves, but to all those everywhere who hate that nation.

I had no notion of conforming to please the bullies, so I became extra Celtic. I persuaded my mother to get me a Teach-Yourself-Welsh book and started learning a few phrases. I told everyone I was going to become a Celtic philologist when I grew up. I'd never have made it. I found Welsh the most difficult language I've ever tried to learn. Latin and Greek were a doddle in comparison.

In my search for Celtic origins I started to ask my mother about her family. It was then that I found out about my Grandmother being the daughter of a German poet. Beset by the English trying to change me, I clung to my roots. I often think that those who research genealogy (or seek for earlier incarnations) lack security. The times in my life when I've dwelt on matters like these have been my most insecure. At ten, I dug desperately for famous ancestors. My mother genuinely had one in the eighteenth century, the hymn writer, William Williams of Pantycelyn. I quoted the phrases used of him to my classmates: "The Milton of Wales", "The founder of the Romantic Movement in Wales". Needless to say, as none of them had read Milton or knew what the Romantic Movement was, they only sneered. In desperation I dug up another lesser ancestor on the other side who had fought with Nelson.

In the process of finding about my reputable ancestors, I also found out about the other kind. I soon heard all about Uncle Sam. I learnt early on that I had the same thumbs as the black sheep of the family, a very bad sign. Uncle Sam had joined the army at twelve – he was big for his age – under the assumed name of John Thomas. He had fought in the Zulu War and been present in the Boxer

Rebellion. His whole life was like a history of late nineteenth and early twentieth century War. Wherever in the world there'd been a famous confrontation in that period, he was there. He was particularly proud of having been one of the few survivors of Rorke's Drift. He had spent years in India, Africa, Shanghai and America. He had even become an American citizen, a fact he forgot to mention when he came back and collected his old age pension. Worst of all he had been put in prison for bigamy. Both wives came to collect him at the door of Swansea gaol, but he told them he didn't want either of them and disappeared to some war or other, somewhere in the world. When my mother knew him he was a very old man, with vivid stories to tell. His handsome looks had gone. One of his eyes had fallen out during a shipwreck and been pushed back slightly out of place. He was a great joker and a great drinker. One of her early recollections was of him having delirium tremens in her Gran's kitchen, going for the little blue devils with a hammer. Another was of him going to the pub with a needle and thread hanging out of his trousers. He pretended he'd sat on it and was in agony until the barmaid pulled it out for him. He was not a chapelgoer like the rest of the family. While they trekked off to the Plymouth Brethren services he'd sit at home quietly reading the *News of the World*. When he was old and sick a pious parson visited him. Hearing he'd come from a certain village he asked: "Did you ever hear the great John Williams preach?" John Williams had been a renowned preacher of saintly character who died young while helping cholera victims during an epidemic. Uncle Sam answered: "Yes, he was my father!"

Once I got my parents talking about their families, there followed an endless string of anecdotes. Mum told me endless stories she'd heard from her adoptive grandmother, tales of Corpse Candles seen in the River Towey. Dad's memories were more reputable. Amersham was a place where everyone was well-to-do. The story of his I liked best was that of him caught peeing in a wood by a Master of Hounds. "Seen him? Seen him?" the man shouted while Dad's golden stream continued. "Seen who?" "The fox, you fool!" Either from a love of animals or resentment at being called a fool, Dad sent the whole hunt in the opposite direction. Dad had probably been mistaken for a yokel. He could put on a very fair imitation of one. While he'd spent all of his working life going into London, there was an undefinable air of the country about him. When my mother first met him she believed he had another woman or a wife stashed away because of his frequent excuses: "I can't see you this weekend because I've got to feed my chickens." His home had been registered as a farm during the War for tax purposes. The only snag was having to provide a certain quota of eggs. Vic and Andrew offloaded this task on to Dad. He had a kind of affinity with fowls. In one particular pair of trousers that had frayed turn-ups he looked rather like a large, lost Buff Orpington. He usually dressed in thick Harris tweed suits. He used to send in his measurements and get them made to order. The first time he did this he was sent back a curt note saying: "Dear Sir, you are a physical impossibility!" He had muddled his waist with his inside leg or something. After that, he paid a professional tailor a pound to measure him and write the results in the correct place on the form. He loved one subtle blue grey houndstooth check so much that he wore it into holes. As he bent over in the garden his testicles would pop out through an aperture in the seat. Mum failed to persuade him he was flashing until she held a large mirror behind him to prove her point.

Dad often dreamed of retirement and keeping hens or geese again. It never happened. He had enjoyed keeping geese particularly. He used to defend his birds fiercely when any neighbours criticised the noise. "They thought you were going to steal their eggs," he'd say accusingly. He also enjoyed feeding them on the side of the garden that abutted a school. The boys got a lot of fun out of it the day their master declaimed: "What did Caesar say?" during a Latin lesson, only to be drowned by a volley of honking and hissing.

Dad had always been a good boy in the schools he attended. He couldn't recollect being punished for anything. Yet he enjoyed the rebellions of others, particularly the boy who kicked his headmaster up the bum while he stooped to choose a cane, then departed through the French windows never to return.

From my mother's and father's stories I picked out role models – Uncle Sam, the kicking boy, Dad as he misled the hunt. It was always the rebels not the conformists that appealed. Dad told other stories about army life that did not strike a chord. I failed to see any charm in his story of how a large delivery of potatoes was secured to feed the army. He had a kind of romantic liking for large quantities of male company that left my mother and myself wondering, at a later stage, whether he was not a closet homosexual. For most of his life he had been a member of the Territorials. His army experience secured him a good rank during the war, acting Major, teaching others how to fight.

When I was ten he became chaplain to the Sea Scouts in Southall. Every Friday night he went down to spend time with them. Mum was quite glad to get him from under her feet once a week. Dad hated the late night involved. By the time he'd caught the 207 bus back, it was impossible to get to bed before 9.30. We saw a kind of love light in his eyes as he talked of "the boys" and uttered clichés about "keeping them off the streets". Probably everyone in youth work has this element of closet, if not overt, paedophilia.

One night he took me along and I played on the assault course and tried to blow a bugle. I had become interested in music again and at last I had got my piano lessons. I loved my teacher, Miss Hett. She was blind and gentle and one of the very few teachers who liked me. Perhaps not being able to see me had something to do with it.

Another teacher who liked me, eventually, was Miss Ashley. She did not like me at ten though. At this stage she taught us gardening. Whether gardening or not, Miss Ashley had a tweed jacket with leather patches on the elbows, and the lowest tits I've seen. Although they didn't stick out far, they were very long. She could literally have tucked them in her belt. We all used to enjoy speculating on what they looked like bare. She was Miss Harold's bosom friend. They lived next door to each other. In later years we children tried to decide whether Miss Harold or Miss Ashley was the butch dyke. We assumed it was our Head, as Miss Ashley did wear makeup and leave off the tweed jackets for parents' days. Years later, I became friendly with Lorraine Molins from the year above, who is now an actress and comedienne. Her mother had shared the same daily as Miss Harold and was told of notes put under the pyjama case from Miss Ashley. The notes began "Dear Bugsy"... If only I'd known that in my schooldays...

At ten, I was completely unaware of the term lesbian. Some theorists argue that early sex education makes children experiment. Yet I experimented with another girl without either of us having heard the terms "lesbian" or "dildo".

Some of our friendships are acquired by proximity. I didn't particularly like this girl, as she was not intelligent. Her parents used to put her on a Green Line from Bucks. The bus got to Ealing so early that she had to wait nearly an hour before school was open. My mother told hers that she could spend that time at our house. So, a new friendship of sorts was born. At first we played card games or fried eggs on my toy stove. Before long, my new-found friend suggested something else. We had both acquired a vague knowledge of the facts of life by then. We both thought that willies were long red things that men stuck up women after which they invariably had babies. We knew none of the subtler points and had not even realised that an erection might be a necessary part of the progress. I had seen only one flasher, in a local park. His member was long red and dangly, the way I thought they all were. It probably had something to do with the cold wind on that day.

My new found friend said that she knew a girl who'd made herself a willy and tried what it felt like on her friend. Of course I saw through the "a friend did it" routine. I'd said much the same when I wanted to test my parents' reaction after I'd been taken short in Halleloopah. Still, the idea did sound interesting. My mother had a big bag of patchwork material and I found a scrap of cherry red material that seemed fitted for the task. I stitched it into a sort of tube, turned it inside out and filled it with kapok and seamed up the end before attaching it to a harness made of old knicker elastic. My friend and I took turns to try it on one another. A vibrator would certainly have been more hygienic had we known about such things or had enough pocket money to buy one. While I did find the act arousing, it was more by fantasy than through the physical side. In my mind I connected it to "The Wedding Night" with some future man. The actual willy was such a limp one that neither of us achieved more than about an inch of penetration in our virgin fannies. We continued to experiment externally, trickling olive oil or water on our genitals or breasts. At ten and eleven, respectively, we only had the beginnings of the latter. We both felt if we massaged each others' enough they might grow.

Eventually the Green Line times were changed, and, after about a year and a half our experimentation had to cease. About two years later I continued not dissimilar investigations with two other girls, although most of these were confined to the breasts. I can honestly say I've never had an orgasm with a girl, but I did enjoy the preliminary stages.

There was one tricky moment when my mother nearly discovered what I was up to. She'd probably have been horrified if she found out. Mum had always been an inveterate reader of diaries and searcher of drawers. Eventually she found my limp red cherry willy on elastic, tucked into the side cupboard of my dressing table. "What's this?" she demanded. Fortunately it was not at that stage stained enough to reveal my infamy. I thought the best policy was not to deny, but only to tell her part of the truth. I settled for telling her I'd made it so that I could dress up as a flasher to amuse my friends. That seemed a reasonably plausible explanation, so she left it at that.

Chapter Fifteen: Firebrands

I WAS GIVEN a bike for passing my Eleven-plus. Before that I only had a blue tin scooter. One leg used to get very tired going round the block. Although I later became ambidextrous, I didn't seem to be fully so at that stage. My mother said I was always stretching out my left hand for things as a baby. When I started to use cutlery, she'd put my spoon on the right, hoping to convert me. It worked, and I became officially right-handed by the time I went to school. Somewhere inside me though, there was a left-hander waiting to get out. I can do almost everything with either hand now. I can certainly draw and paint well with both. At art school I often drew the left side of the model with my left and the right with my right, sometimes working with both simultaneously. When I drink from a cup, sometimes I pick it up with one hand, sometimes with the other. Invariably, lipstick gets left on both sides of the china.

But my left hand is not all that sure for handwriting. My right is only marginally better. In fact I loathe writing anything by hand. After a page or so, I always suffer from severe writer's cramp. Even as a child I preferred a typewriter and now I'm very happy with computers and willing to learn any technology that saves me from writing longhand.

Unfortunately for me, Miss Harold and many of her staff loved the business of writing by hand. We were all made to learn the rudiments of calligraphy. We even got a lecture from Miss Harold on how the ancient Mesopotamians started it all with cuneiform. If she could have forced us all to write cuneiform she would. Bugger the Mesopotamians for that, I thought. Even now, I can't take to them.

Miss Brook, another lover of handwriting, had taught it for the last two years. Needless to say I was punished more often than most for my poor writing when she was in charge. In Writing lessons we had to trace a poem off a card, transfer it to paper then ink over it with our dip pens, using thick and thin strokes in the right places. Somewhere along the line I always made a blot and used to be made to start all over again ad infinitum. I still feel physically sick at the thought of "Oh to be in England" and "Pippa's Song". They were the two poems I fucked-up on most. I can still feel the sensations of writer's cramp and the mess of ink all over my hands when I think of their words. I never felt the same level of hatred for poems I had

merely been forced to learn. In fact, I wouldn't have minded learning poems at all, if I had been allowed merely to remember the
words and recite them. Haberdashers', with its rigorous discipline,
asked more of its pupils. Under Miss Davies we all had to write out
the poems or passages of prose we had memorised. We then lost a
mark for every minor error of punctuation – if we had a semi-colon
instead of a full stop, for instance. It's not a way to make children
like literature.

We had to use dip pens until a form or two into our secondary
school. Even fountain pens were thought decadent. I can still
remember my intense feelings of hatred for the piece of yellow
wood that held my nib. When you broke a nib, you could buy a new
one for a penny from Miss Overton's store cupboard. Breaking one
a term was considered normal. I always broke several more. The
school ink was a murky navy blue, adulterated with God knows
what. There were always strange particles and hair in it that stuck
on my nib and made blots on the paper. I knew in my heart that I
was doomed to failure every time I started to write at school. At
home, I quietly used a fountain pen and the teachers usually didn't
notice the difference.

I have sometimes wondered what it is that I hate so much about
writing by hand. I have come to the conclusion that I feel it's healthy
for both hands and both sides of the brain to be functioning simultaneously. I've noticed that people usually function one way or the
other, often according to their profession. A pianist and a typist
work with both hands at once, while most artists and many writers
work with one only. I consider that imperfect. It seems a wrong,
one-sided way of working. I believe the flow of thought from brain
to hands should be fully symmetrical.

Cycling as opposed to scooting with one leg felt like a healthy
symmetrical activity. Having my own transport liberated me. I very
soon learned to ride the bike, wobbling along the pavements. I
should have been on the road as it was not really a children's bike. I
was tall enough for the smallest size of adult model. My father tried
riding my new bike too, although it was definitely too small for him.
He had to turn his knees outward to stop them hitting the handle-
bars.

On my first day out I careered into a couple who were
canoodling down the pavement and blasted them apart. Fortunately

they were in love and far too happy to give me a ticking off. Within a day or two, the bike was under control and I was riding on the roads. At that stage I didn't go very far. Three or four miles would exhaust me. I usually only went in search of new parks to play in. There was one with a huge slide in North Acton and a smaller one in Springfield Gardens. The North Acton playground was better equipped. I liked going down the slide headfirst or climbing its metal poles. I was beginning to find that I could climb a pole or rope easily, although I was not particularly good at sports otherwise. Only three of us in the year could climb ropes, myself, Angela Goto and Ruth Flavin. The other two were both athletic, yet I, unaccountably, had the same monkey skill. At the end of every term we'd have a game of shipwreck in the gym. Those who could climb a rope would always win if the chaser couldn't.

The slide in North Acton was eventually closed when a child fell headfirst off it on to the concrete. I was there just after she'd been bundled into the ambulance to be treated for concussion. My trips took some time, so they were usually made at the weekend.

On weekdays evenings, I sometimes visited Springfield Gardens, which was only half a mile away. It was less well equipped than the North Acton park, but the children were more fun. The swings were boxed-in children's ones and the seesaw and roundabout were old and splintery. It was just into the area where Acton divided from Ealing. Most of the kids were from Acton and did not have the same aspirations as the young Habs girls. They were certainly not the types my mother would have chosen for me. But I always had an instinct that forced me to look further afield than the safe bourgeois hothouse atmosphere of schools such as Haberdashers'. It's the same instinct that drives me now to look at the red-light district of any city as well as the cultural sights. Haberdashers with its single sex, single class ambience gave a narrow and damaging view of the way things are. We were all programmed to get good results in exams, then go on to university. After that there would be a good safe job and marriage for those that wanted it. Our sights were set no higher or lower than that. No other aim was thought acceptable. Such an education was to prove no real preparation for the world outside, a world that is much more extreme in terms of richness and poverty, wisdom and ignorance.

The main charm of Springfield Gardens was the badinage

between the sexes. An Indian boy came up to me as soon as I appeared and said: "I'd like to stick my carrot in your turnip field." I don't know quite why a London-born Asian used a metaphor like that. I don't think either of us had seen carrot or turnip fields in our lives. He also offered me ten shillings for a sight of my knickers. Being a fool about money I showed them for free. My mother had always said I shouldn't be prudish about being seen in them, a phrase I took quite literally. Looking back on it, I assume she was referring to changing amongst other girls at school, rather than flashing at strangers. Quite what that boy got out of seeing my distinctly unattractive navy knitted knickers (as ordered by Miss Harold) I can't imagine.

At ten I was beginning to be more fashion conscious (except about knickers). I had my long hair in a heavy plait and wore shifts up to my bottom. It was the days of the mini-skirt. Mum used to buy a yard of some exotic material as a remnant and seam it up the side, with a little slit at the thigh so that I could walk easily without the dress riding up. My favourite was a lurid jungly print in shades of emerald green and olive. It was a sort of high sheen cotton satin and glistened in the sun. I wore that dress to the park many times and drew the admiration of another slightly older boy. John had been to borstal, the other girls told me admiringly. One night they called for me at my home, to persuade me to come and play. They confided he'd bought me a bunch of flowers, daffodils. The flowers never materialised. Shortly after this, John, who was fourteen, turned up with one arm in a sling, pretending he'd broken it. He asked me to reach in his pocket to find his handkerchief. The pocket had no bottom. Presumably he'd cut that out. I stopped before I reached what he obviously wanted me to hold. I wasn't that keen on John, although I wouldn't have minded the flowers.

Most of the girls were ten to thirteen and most of the boys were in their early teens. There was one very young kid though. She was only seven and always dressed in pink. She used to hang out by the Gents and sometimes disappeared inside with boys of sixteen or so. "She sucks men's willies," I was told. I told my Mum about that because it seemed a bizarre activity. I never connected it with sex. She wasn't married after all. It seemed more like eating worms, or something. Mum assumed I was lying, which may have been just as well for the kid. If she'd believed me she'd have had to alert the authorities and the child would probably have been taken into care immediately. While child abuse was certainly going on, it seems possible to me that the child's willing sucking of cocks might actually have done her less harm than being put into a home. Nobody seemed to be intimidating her. Her disappearances into the Gents were obviously quite voluntary.

It was outside this particular lavatory that I saw my first flasher. He was to be the first of many. I am probably not exaggerating to say that I've seen a thousand since in various parts of the globe. I sometimes refer to myself as "The face that launched a thousand flashers".

One Sunday afternoon, a local evangelical group descended. The "Firebrands" invited us all to Sunday School. Almost everyone, including the little cocksucker, trouped off. We were willing to try anything after all. I continued with the Firebrands for a couple of months. I quite enjoyed singing choruses like: "I will make you fishers of men." It was there that I first saw a Down's Syndrome kid. It was only years after that I realised what was wrong with her. At the time, I was just slightly surprised that she was allowed to sit on the table displaying her knickers and that her rather poor drawings were always praised. It's curious, children often don't see each other as handicapped the way adults do.

Chapter Sixteen: I Learn Something at School

ON MY TENTH birthday I indulged myself with a really revolting party. I had acquired all sorts of jokes from a fascinating but expensive toyshop called *Confiserie Française*. My friends loved the whoopee cushion which I had planted on a mock throne. The party was one long romp with games like "Pin the Pants on the Headmistress". One of my friends was being stripped forcibly by a gang of us. We had promised her threepence if she kept silent during the process. My mother came in and spoilt that game, unaware of the rage of the girl who had just lost her threepence. Only one girl was not amused, Rosemary Lethem. She was clever but so sober in manner that she wasn't well liked. Some of us suspected that she might be years older in fact.

That party seemed to be the last happy time for a long while. I sometimes feel that something went profoundly wrong with my education between the years of seven and ten. I was seriously bored because I wasn't actually learning anything new at school, but that was only part of the picture. My mother had let me read any book that interested me for years. Between her and my father there were about four thousand books on different subjects at home. She had a detailed knowledge of English literature and Greek and Roman mythology, which she was able to pass on to me. Sometimes she read aloud, at other times I preferred to read to myself. Both she and my father also knew a lot about religious subjects. There were several hundred theological books, about a dozen different translations of the Bible, the Koran and even the Book of Mormon, all readily available. My father was well versed in history and general knowledge and I picked up things like basic maths pretty quickly. I also taught myself the subjects in which my parents were lacking, natural history and music.

After all that, school was bound to be boring. I had hoped to learn Latin young. I heard some nine-year olds reciting it when I was seven. Even in their childish voices it had a heavy sonorous magical sound. I assumed we would begin Latin classes at nine, but waited in vain. What I had heard was indeed Latin, but it was only the verses of the school song, which we were required to learn parrot fashion, with a brief summation of the meaning, long before we could construe them word by word.

I got Mum to teach me a little real Latin at about the time my grandfather died. I hadn't been as close to him as I was to Gran. He was a bit tired and crotchety by the time I was born. His death was an excuse for another visit to Mumbles, the trip that won me Miss Overton's scorn. Mum as before, thought I ought to see the body. I still remember how respectable he looked in his Paisley dressing gown.

There was no need for a will as my grandparents had given away everything they owned in the years leading up to their death. Their house had been sold to my aunt and the money divided between the other two children. After the funeral, Auntie Dor, who had been Granddad's favourite, consoled herself the Welsh way by a manic bout of cleaning and turning unwanted possessions out. Their childhood piano went to a mission. A few coverlets went back with us as well as a hastily salvaged pile of books. Mum greatly regretted the haste with which the books were being chucked out. Some had been her childhood favourites – old Sunday School prizes, books of sermons and illustrated copies of the Pilgrim's Progress. One of the books, a very old Greek Testament printed by Baskerville, came away minus its top cover. It would have been valuable if it had been complete but the cover was swept away in the great clean up. Although I couldn't read Greek at that stage I greatly admired the look of the script. I also found Mum's old Latin schoolbook at Gran's – I still thought of the Mumbles house as Gran's although it now belonged to my aunt. I got Mum to start teaching me, but she ran out of patience by the second declension. It's just as well she never went in for it professionally, she would have made a very poor teacher. I found that again when I tried to learn German from her years later. She would become angry at every question. I always found I couldn't remember anything unless I knew the reason behind it. I also wanted to know the exceptions to every rule. Some teachers found my constant questioning positive, others, like my mother, loathed it.

With nothing to learn, all that was to be had from school was discipline. If I'd had pats on the back for my creative endeavours I would have hated that less. I began to have a little hope for the future when Miss Overton taught us a little French. I went home to my parents and said excitedly, "I've learned something in school at last!"

To be fair to Miss Overton, she did do some positive things. She read good books to us, The Hobbit, for instance. It wasn't her fault that I'd heard most of them before, read by my mother. Teaching us a little French before it officially became part of the school curriculum was also a good idea. Thanks to her spell in the Sorbonne, Miss Overton's accent was reasonably authentic. We learned some basic phrases, words to do with the classroom and also two or three songs: "Alouette", "Frère Jacques" and a ghastly counting one called "Un elephant se trompe". We kids speculated on exactly what sort of mistake the elephant had made. I was perfectly certain it had left a steaming pile in the midst of the circus ring. I had never seen a real circus. My father was particularly against them, assuming they involved cruelty galore.

We didn't receive homework regularly at this stage, but we were often given projects for the holidays and half-term weekends. My colourful and excellent Christmas stories had received grudging marks and comments. At half term, in the Spring, there came a chance which could, I felt, win Miss Overton to my side. We had been asked to prepare a list of all the French names of animals we could find. It was a sort of competition for which we were promised a prize. The term "animal" was used loosely. Almost anything non-human and animate could be included. I worked like a beaver. (I'm sure he was on my list.) My mother had Fontaine's fables in French, so my first step was to go through those. Then I wrote down a list of every species I could think of and worked through a dictionary looking them up, all the way from Aardvark to Zebra.

When I got to school my list was several pages long. Most of the other girls had come up with twelve words or so, obvious farmyard animals and pets. Some had not bothered at all. Miss Overton used the latter point as an excuse to cancel the competition, once she saw that her least favourite pupil was all set to win. It wouldn't be fair, she said, to hold the competition, when some children hadn't even started their lists. "Fair" of course did not come into it.

At seven, I had been humiliated by being sent to a psychologist for a most trivial offence. At nine I was mentally tortured for a whole term by a disturbed teacher. At ten, I had to put up with a lack of praise for good essays and sneers at my Welshness. I learnt from Miss Williams and Miss Harold that cleverness combined with slight naughtiness might be defined as insanity. I learnt from Miss

Brook that some individuals can hate you on sight and persecute you for no good reason. From Miss Overton I learnt that things like race or poverty can prejudice a person against another. Apart from a few dozen French words, these were the sum total of the things I learned from my primary school. This were to have a deep effect on my psyche.

I sometimes tell people that I was totally depressed from the time I entered school until I was thirty or so. That's more or less true, but I didn't enter the deepest numbest phase of it until I was ten. Under Miss Brook's cruel treatment, I was at least able to fight back in a way. I found that I was able to persuade the other girls, one by one, of my innocence. Similarly I had convinced the psychologists of my sanity. Because Miss Overton's treatment was less extreme, there was no similar measure that could be taken.

The one tiny bit of comfort in this period came from my winning a book token in Ealing library's children's poetry competition. It gave a tiny piece of proof that my writing was good and that someone who was not judging me by my accent and lack of exotic holidays might see that.

I wish now that my parents had brought me up with a television. Being poor we looked for things we could avoid without losing face. We had no car, but we could claim it was healthier to walk. We had no fridge, but we could argue that it meant that we bought fresh food all the time and didn't keep leftovers. We got most Brownie points of all by having no television. Although none of the other parents were prepared to do without their sets, they conceded that it might have been better for their children to spend all their time reading instead. In some ways though, I believe that the lack of a television did me harm. I knew little about popular culture, which is a loss socially. More importantly I did not have access to the equivalent of that library competition. Television gives many children the chance to shine by appearing on programmes or sending in their paintings or poems. I might have received more fairness from judges who were not part of the repressive Haberdashers' system.

It's curious how later parts of my life have mirrored my troubled early years at school. Haberdashers' has its parallel in the literary world. While some arbiters of taste are as impartial as Miss Davies, others, like Miss Overton, feel I'm not from the right background, and yet others, like Miss Brook, quite simply hate me on sight.

Literature is a curiously restricted world compared to the other arts. There is far less tolerance of sexuality, the adult equivalent of "naughtiness". My later promiscuity was castigated in reviews. This would never happen in the worlds of painting or music. Somehow literature retains its school-like quality.

In the same way that I got the girls on my side, one by one, I can win readers. When I perform my poetry, most of the audience is on my side. It's only when I have to deal with editors and publishers that I find myself, uncomfortably, in the school situation. Newspaper editors love to make corrections to a writer's articles. Annoyingly, they sometimes even put bad grammar in, or change the tenor of a review from bad to good, or vice versa. I have the pages to prove it.

It's interesting to speculate on what a friend of mine would call "roads not travelled". At eight, with my long hair, I modelled myself on Alice and taught myself to play chess from a book. I had also read a lot of the major classics and learned the names of many plants in Latin. What if that clever child had been praised for her work at nine and ten, instead of the treatment she received? Would I have grown cleverer? Possibly not. I know for sure though that I would have been happier and nicer to other people. By the end of Miss Overton's form I had settled into a leaden depression that was to last for a large portion of my life. What was the point in working hard, I reasoned. What was the point in trying to please? Whatever efforts I made seemed doomed to failure. I soon ceased to try at all.

Gradually I began to offload all the tasks I could on to my mother. My wrists ached when I wrote, so I persuaded her to take dictation. That was the first step. In the following year I was to go further and she was cajoled into writing some of my essays. She was far from being the only parent to take on this task. The teachers little realised that they were often marking the work of parents rather than children. Some of us, myself included, couldn't have cared less if we were expelled. We weren't going to make any efforts to stay and so our parents worriedly composed essays or added up columns of figures on our behalf. The parents began to take pride in getting B for their essays, or else resented getting a mark less than the others. A good many of us were cheats, but we were forced into it by a system that loaded us with impossible amounts of homework. Our parents covered for us, desperate to keep us in a good school that would improve our chances of getting to university later on. My parents weren't particularly scientific so help was only given for English, History and Scripture. The doctors' daughters in the class often got more help for science and less for the arts. I still did my own poetry or tackled any essay subject that really interested me. But I usually lay on my back to dictate. Life felt a little easier that way.

My mother's other effort to help me was stitching a little red pair of kneepads, faked to look like the school hymnbook. Armed with my hassock I could kneel on the splintery parquet floor with less pain than the other girls. Miss Harold always made morning prayers last for about half an hour. We stood for the hymns, sat cross-legged for the reading and knelt for interminable prayers.

Miss Harold fancied herself as an orator. She would roll up her eyes and emphasise certain words like "the glorious resurrection" when she was praying. Miss Ashley told us this was a proof of her piety. We saw it rather differently as we knelt in agony on that splintery floor.

Chapter Seventeen: The Pinner Set

THAT SUMMER I went to Hastings for my holiday. I thoroughly enjoyed myself, as my tastes were more plebeian than Miss Overton's. We stayed in a tiny flatlet in Cornwallis Road and I could hear the seagulls all night. I did not realise then that a large part of my life was to be spent in Hastings and that I would come to know certain members of the seagull population very well.

I swam by the pier and frightened my mother by hiring a float and going out to the end of it. She could see fifteen or twenty feet of green water around me as she gestured me back inland. But by now I was a good swimmer and in no real danger. I'd passed my bronze medallion easily in doggy paddle. I never took to the school form of breaststroke and used no proper technique until my mid-teens when I discovered the rarely used sidestroke and took to it. I still swim that way. It's perfect for use in the sea as opposed to swimming baths. You can align your body to the waves and the wind, adapting your position in the water to every incoming swell.

In the evenings I frequented the arcades with Mum in attendance. I enjoyed gambling on the penny principle. Fortunately I've always been too mean to take it to a higher level. I found one arcade where you could bet on film stars. The lights would go round and settle on one or other. It was a very old machine, which favoured names like Ava Gardner. I worked out a system and always bet on the stars who were rated at tuppence. They came up oftenest. To my delight I left after an hour or two with a couple of shillings' profit.

Mum had a few pounds to subsidise Dad's usual very basic allowance. It was a little bit of the tiny sum of money her parents gave away before they died. She fed us lavishly with pints of prawns and honeycomb and cream. I had never tasted honey from the comb before and I instantly became addicted. I still occasionally treat myself to a comb from a local beekeeper.

Hastings also had pleasant memories for my father, although he was left in Ealing working and minding the cats on this occasion. During the First World War in his childhood he had spent a long period of time there with his mother. His father wasn't at all anxious to be with her at that period. He kept pretending he couldn't get any leave from the Army to come and see her. It seems very probable that she was having an affair at the time. She was escorted every-

where by a local man called Harris. He used to row her and my
father out so far to sea, that Dad swore he could hear the guns in
France. I've always taken that tale with a pinch of salt though.

I still have one photo from my happy week in Hastings. I was
wearing the jungle-printed shift that was my usual uniform for
Springfield Gardens. My hair was in a heavy plait and I was looking
lovingly into the eyes of a monkey in a woolly jersey. I had him cuddled in my arms like a tiny baby.

By the time I was due to go back to school I had decided to cut
my hair. The hairdresser chopped it off into a sort of bob. Nobody
could pull my plaits any longer and I would no longer have the horror of trying to comb out the tangles every time it was washed.

When I entered the upper school, there were a lot of new
pupils. Some of those who had not won scholarships, together with
the few that could not pass the entrance exam left Haberdashers at
the end of primary school. Most of the new girls were reasonably
likeable but I didn't make close friends amongst them. It must have
been rather hard for them to enter a school where at least half the
girls knew each other already. There was one group that became fast
friends travelling the same route in the morning. They mostly came
from Pinner or thereabouts. Within a year or two several of them
had lost their virginity, although one admitted she did not know if
she had or not, as she was drunk at the time. I'd only been through
Pinner on the train, but reckoned it must be a very debauched place.
I asked my father about it. He sniggered and talked about a river
called the Mighty Pin that goes underground in times of trouble. I
urged him to take me to see the Mighty Pin, but he thought it might
well be underground at that moment, and even if it wasn't it was
only a few inches wide. Both as a child and adult, I found irony the
hardest form of humour to understand.

By the time we were twelve or so, my friend of the lesbian tendencies had left me for the Pinner set. The parents of one of them
had offered a lift, which saved her getting the Green Line every
morning. I was rather relieved. We were always quarrelling by then.
She used to chant: "Taffy was a Welshman, Taffy was a thief" or yell
"Welsh cow!" to bait me. She usually did this at lunch, attempting
to wind me up in front of the other girls. She invariably succeeded.
On one occasion we were both monitors, setting the place to rights
when everyone had left, so I used the opportunity to christen her

with a water jug. Fortunately it was one of the art mistresses who caught me, so my only punishment was mopping up.

Three of the Pinner set were extremely tall and plump. They must have been five feet ten. They were only twelve, but looked years older, so much so that one was offered a job working as a stripper in Ealing fair. She was sorely tempted. While most of us had a tiny amount of breast by now we were slightly jealous of the girls who had big obvious ones. My first bra was a white lacy one given to me by Auntie Dor. It was 32A and I had a hard job filling it.

Our classroom in the lower fourth was just off the main hall where we had Prayers. School life seemed more mobile than before. Our form mistress rarely taught us and lessons were all over the place – other classrooms, the Scripture room, Science labs. As we trouped from one end of the school to the other we'd creep up on the girl in front and try to undo her bra if she was wearing one.

We had a new English mistress, Miss Everett. She reminded me awfully of one of my tabby cats, Esther. Tess had so many sons and daughters by now, that I often turned to the Bible with a pin for picking their names. One poor little black and white kitten got called Mephibosheth as a result. Esther, or Eggy for short, was beautifully marked with clear grey and black stripes like a glittering mackerel. I had taught her to prance on end as I sang "Stand up, stand up for Jesus" as learned from the Firebrands. Everyone thought her a very pious cat and did not realise she would as easily have stood up for Satan if I'd clicked my fingers at the relevant word. I am convinced that most animals have strains of other species in their ancestry. Personally I believe in bestiality rather than evolution. Eggy's alien ancestor was definitely a skunk. Or possibly she was a reincarnation of one. Her sister, Clarissa, after all, was much more like a squirrel. Eggy had a filthy knack of raising her tail when nervous and spraying a fine mist on whoever happened to be standing near. It wasn't urine. It smelt much much worse. Fortunately, I've never met any other cat capable of such vileness. It was a trick all of her own. We didn't get her put down for it; we simply tried very hard not to make her nervous often. She was much stouter than Miss Everett, but it was something about the face that was similar. Eggy had tiny superfluous whiskers as well as her main set. They stuck out all around her chin. She also had a habit of screwing up her eyes like a myopic woman. I brought a troupe of girls to look at that cat and they all saw the resemblance. And so our poor harmless English teacher got christened Eggy Everett.

Miss Everett was a decent enough teacher on the whole. Like many of those who teach English Literature, she also had aspirations to write. She used to go to a creative writing class once a week with the history teacher, Miss Oyler.

One of the essays I wrote for her involved seeing my own future. I realised that my mother would have to die eventually, so I asked her what she was least likely to die of. She answered "TB". I put in the essay that my mother had died of TB. I felt strongly that words had power and putting down any disease that might be likely to kill her could have a very unlucky result. I wasn't going to say cancer, because I'd seen Gran go that way. Nor was I going to say a bad heart, because that was somehow more possible. TB was just an impossible joke as an end for my fat mother, according to my line of reasoning.

I decided that in my old age I would be in Ireland by the sea. This earned me some loss of marks from Miss Everett as she was anti-Irish, it turned out. I presumed by then that I would be married and had to invent a suitable name for my husband. I chose an unlikely and fanciful one, Ethelred Chintz. I did not realise that a man who did not change a name like that by deed poll would, almost certainly, be gay. As yet, I had no concept or knowledge of homosexuals, in spite of my own experience with my friend and in spite of the many camp friends of my father who still passed through our house dressed up in bishop's robes.

Why did I like the name Ethelred Chintz and even blush at its sound? I suppose that the surname came from my love of fabrics. Mum would take me remnant hunting in Bentalls in Ealing Broadway. My imaginary love's Christian name came from my liking for history. Since learning a few runes at six, I'd been interested in the Saxons. It hadn't dawned on me that they were the natural enemies of the Celts and that I couldn't really side with both. I particularly liked the name of one king, Ethelred the Unready. He occurred on a list of English rulers on one of my mother's tea towels. She explained again and again that Unready in Saxon meant "uncounselled", but I still had another kind of vision of him. My mother was always complaining in the morning: "You're not ready!" I was usually half-asleep and too busy playing with dildoes, cats and magic tricks from the *Confiserie Française to* get my act together and go to school. Ethelred obviously had similar problems to mine, I thought. I had every sympathy with a man who was unready permanently. It was years before I read about Ethelred in detail and found out that he was in reality a right pain in the arse and had started his unlovely career by crapping in the font while being baptised. They don't put things like that in school textbooks, unfortunately.

Apart from the imaginary Ethelred Chintz, my only fancy had been for the brother of one of the other girls. The year before, Frances Packman had invited us to a party in Uxbridge or thereabouts. Her brother was handsome and vivacious and a few years older than us. We all corporately fell for him as he helped us play games like passing matchboxes on the end of our noses. Perhaps he revelled in our feminine adoration, or perhaps he simply liked kids.

I was beginning to play with magic tricks. I hadn't the patience to practice long enough for serious feats of prestidigitation, but enjoyed the lesser sort of conjuring. I liked to make my own adaptations. A little gadget like a tiny mangle was intended for changing paper into pound notes. The real pound note was hidden inside and rolled out as the paper rolled in. I changed its use and would insert a fully clothed picture of a teacher who'd come out naked the other side. I enjoyed making and adapting things. In Miss Overton's class I'd acted the Dragon fighting against St. George. The head was a box covered with green silk with holes for eyes. I was prouder of the wings. For these I'd used an ancient large City businessman's umbrella that had lain in our hall for years. The fabric was so old that pinpricks of light shone through it when you held it up. It had long been past any usefulness. Once the stick was taken away and the rest cut in half it did admirably for wings. The jointed result could be made to creak and flap infernally by pulling a string. I'd always been drawn to that umbrella. As a very young child I christened it "The umbrella of Night filled with holes of Hope."

I toyed with the idea of being a conjuror and even taught myself a tiny amount of ventriloquy. I sometimes sat Eggy upright on my lap and spoke for her. I was often rewarded with her skunk trick. I gave all the other cats voices too. Who needs a ventriloquist's doll when they've got a cat?

I learnt one or two simpler tricks with string or paper from old Rupert Bear annuals. I read those to a late age whenever I felt in need of a little comfort. I particularly liked the rhyming couplets beneath the pictures. Besides, his parents reminded me strongly of mine. Just as Miss Everett resembled Eggy, my parents were like two great anthropomorphic bears in loose Fifties clothing. It was now the mid-Sixties, but they'd managed to keep clear of short skirts and Beatles culture. Mum slightly despised the parents who went for all that.

Odd relations had taught me card tricks too. I tried all these out on my friend in the morning when we weren't doing other things. I had a wonderful Halloween party planned. All the new girls were to be invited. My pièce de resistance was to be hiding behind a curtain while girls sat looking in a mirror for their husbands. I had rigged up a string on which were to be lowered a series of horrible masks. A greenish decayed picture of Odysseus was easily the most frightening when seen in a half-light. My dildo-partner friend divulged all my plans to the class at large and managed to spoil some of them.

When there were new girls to impress I seemed to resort to horror and humour. I had done the same in my first year of primary school. One of my other stunts this time round was writing a short version of the Masque of the Red Death in which I was to play the eponymous disease itself. I wore a sheet toga and stretched a piece of red lace across my face. We performed the play in class. The Dragon followed by the Red Death. Again and again in the years that followed I was to play villains.

Dad threw himself into my Halloween party preparations with enthusiasm. He enjoyed brewing homemade drinks, as he was teetotal. His ginger beer was passable, but some of the others were definitely an acquired taste. He had bought a concentrate of some herbal elixir at Baldwin's health shop in the Elephant and Castle and prepared several gallons of it across a week or so. He labelled the bottles and gallon jars "Witches' Brew". It would have been terribly good for their bowels and complexions, but several kids recoiled from its black, slightly oleaginous appearance. The more adventurous ones tried it before reverting to normal drinks like orange barley.

After all the games were over, when we'd bobbed for apples, roasted chestnuts and looked for our husbands in mirrors and been duly horrified, when everyone was ready to leave, various parents turned up to drive them home. Dad rushed out and offered them all a drink. Barbara Levy's mother, a sophisticated elegant Jewish lady was the only one to say yes. She sat down, obviously hoping for a drop of dry sherry or a glass of wine. I can still remember the look on her face when my father handed her a dripping half-pint glass of his homemade Stygian beverage.

Chapter Eighteen: I Turn Pious

IN THE NEXT year I was to encounter an English teacher who thought I was wonderful. Miss Ashley really appreciated the essays my mother wrote or embellished for me. Even in class I could do no wrong.

Yet, Miss Ashley's adoration was a mixed blessing. I have since told people it was a bit like being friends with Nero. Seneca and Petronius must have gone through much the turmoil that I did. I had learned already, in the days when she taught me gardening, that she was liable to sudden diabolical fits of rage that could be triggered by the most trivial offence. On one occasion I had left my gardening scissors at home, so she decided to let loose the blast of her wrath on me. She came to school next day sporting a piratical patch. She had literally burst a blood vessel in her eye during her fit. I got a bit of respect from my friends for having put the evil eye on her, as it were.

Because of her violent hysterical tendencies I was never able to like Miss Ashley even when she was nice to me and gave me a modern poetry anthology as a present. While I seemed safe from her wrath for the moment, I could hear her shouted sarcasms being heaped on my friends. She was bizarrely strict. The margins on essays had to be measured exactly and ruled in pencil. A deviation of a couple of millimetres would earn you a mark less, as would a margin drawn in ink rather than pencil. The same would happen if you forgot to put a date at the top, or the time you'd taken at the end. We were supposed to take half an hour exactly for an essay. Of course, they always took us, or our parents, much longer. And Mum was always very dispirited if she got a mark or two less than the essay deserved because we'd forgotten the margin or the date.

I am convinced that Miss Ashley's demon rages were the result of sexual frustration. Several other teachers suffered from the same problem. They were not all single. Some of the married ones were every bit as bad as the single. Miss Ashley, however, was quite in a class of her own on the rage front. I am convinced that regular orgasms with "Bugsy" alias Miss Harold, would have kept a smile on her face and also have made her feel that the width of the margin on an essay was not a matter of primary importance in the world scheme of things. Even a little time spent masturbating would have helped her. I know from my own experience that the times when I had no orgasms were the times when I was most apt to take my anger out on other people. While lonely masturbation has a depressing element, it also has a calming effect. Miss Ashley could certainly have done with that. As it was, we were all terrified of her screaming hysterical rages. They made it impossible for anyone to like her. We all knew that we were walking a tightrope in her class. The slightest failing and we'd be met with a tornado.

Dad had a longish stint in a job with an educational paper that involved him in visiting various libraries making précis from books and articles. I went with him in the holidays and read odd books that were available. Sometimes there were only dictionaries or heavy tomes of reference. At lunchtime I was often taken to Chinese restaurants where he'd stretch his luncheon vouchers to a treat for two. We usually managed to pop into a Christopher Wren church also to admire the architecture. In those days, churches were always open. Few are as trusting now.

By eleven I was becoming more religious and spent odd Sundays consumer-testing various churches in London with my father. I had become quite a connoisseur of sermons. He never really felt comfortable with Catholicism, but we visited many other denominations in turn. Sometimes congregations made us welcome, sometimes not. The one where I felt least at home proved to be Crown Court, a particularly elitist Scottish Presbyterian church. All the Scottish snobs of London were in attendance and we had dressed scruffily that day. Thanks to the looks we got, I felt as welcome as a turd on someone's boot by the end of the service. My father never even noticed. He was probably far too used to shocked and perturbed expressions every time he cocked his leg at a lamppost. Bourgeois horror was all water off a duck's back to him.

I consoled myself by going home and imitating the congregation singing the 24th psalm in a strong Scots accent: "The laird's my shepherd" etc. I swear that I heard them sing "laird" rather than lord. Somehow the whole religion of that church seemed more based on the adoration of class than divinity.

I wanted to join a church choir and looked around for a suitable one. I had enjoyed a Mrs. Henry Wood novel called *The Channings* about a choir school. There were also bits about them in William Mayne's books. I would dearly have loved to go to such a school had that been possible. My voice sounded exactly like a prize-winning choirboy's, yet the sexism of the Church made that road impossible for any girl in those days. The best I could do was sing in a local church on Sundays. I was soon taken on at St. Martin's where I rapidly fell in love.

Charles Martin, the object of my adoration, sat halfway down the church with his family. They were all churchgoers, but he and his brother only turned up in the holidays, as they were both at university. Even when he was away I used to get a vicarious thrill out of cycling past his house on the corner of Western Road. I tried to incite my mother to ask his mother round for coffee, but she wouldn't play. It was, of course, an absolute no-hope situation. What decent bloke of twenty would consider taking up with an urchin of twelve?

I watched Charles Martin for many months and tried to ignore the fact that he sometimes had a woman beside him. She must be a long-lost sister, I figured, or a cousin. Funny they were holding hands though. I counted the months till I was sixteen and marriageable. It still seemed an awfully long way ahead.

In the mean time I tried to make myself look as desirable as possible. I had started experimenting with make-up. I ordered a stick from Woman's Own that contained a beige lipstick, blue eye shadow and black mascara all in one. Every single item was the wrong colour for me and the make-up was thick and bad quality. I also painted my toenails lilac. They were clearly visible hanging out of my Scholl sandals as I clacked round the church, processing with the choir. I assumed the whole effect would be irresistible.

I made a new set of friends in the church choir. I particularly liked the Warne boys, Steven and Anthony. One was slightly older, one slightly younger than me. I could probably have got some more real romance going with one or other of them if I hadn't been so intent on my fantasies about Charles Martin.

I got on well too with the adult members of the choir. Officially Archer, the church organist, a dapper likeable Cornishman, ran it. He had a small whisker on the end of his nose. We children convinced ourselves that it waved as he conducted. While Archer was our boss, unofficially, Miss Goodwin, a crippled senior soprano, ruled the roost. She had been a seamstress and still took care of gowns and cassocks. She had got to the age where she could only mouth not sing. She was slightly disapproving of us kids, so we took a certain pleasure when she was done for the opposite of speeding in her motorised invalid carriage. Her offence was going across the traffic lights on Hanger Lane at less than ten miles an hour. But *Goodie* was likeable enough. She could walk but was slow and balanced from one leg to another. Probably these days she'd have been right as rein with hip replacements. Usually she went and sat in the church before the rest of us, not to hold up the procession. The children in the choir had cruel names for the handicapped. One server, who bore the cross occasionally in front of us, was nicknamed *Old Humpy*.

We had a tiny amount of pay in the junior choir. It worked out as about a shilling a service and half a crown for weddings. I saved my money and bought odd treats like board games or a pair of fur-lined leather gloves. We were particularly glad of the half-crowns for weddings. We usually sang *Jesu Joy of Man's Desiring*. I was already beginning to love Bach's soaring passages and wished that we were singing the complicated accompaniment rather than the simple melody line. Brides almost always also chose "Love Divine" not realising that God's love was referred to rather than their own. If the groom was a soldier, a dreadful hymn, "I vow to thee my country" was included. I was becoming quite a connoisseur of hymns and hated the banality of the words and the way they fitted unevenly to the music.

Something about singing at weddings made us all become strangely cynical. We were used to over-hearing congregation members bitch about the dress. It was easy too to spot little rivalries between members of the families on each side of the church. Sometimes the pages played up horribly. We all enjoyed it when one used a polo mint as monocle throughout the service.

One time the junior choir was filled with venom for the bride. Our usual pay was docked by a shilling because she had hired a mannered tenor to sing a perfectly dreadful Ave Maria that began: "You by my side that's how I see us." Of course we were more hurt by the loss of money than the appalling taste of the aria. We would gladly have sung it for half a crown.

I was confirmed at twelve and entered my pious period. Confirmation involved going to the local vicar, George Yeulett, for a few classes. He was short, fat and jolly with a face like an owl. He also had a fat ginger cat. He would never tell me the cat's name, so

I assumed he must have called it something unrepeatable and obscene.

As soon as I was confirmed I started going to church several times a day. I'd go to communion at eight, back home for breakfast, then on to two morning services and back again for evensong. It didn't do me a bit of good. I think I've actually been a much nastier person at the times I've been a Christian. Religion seems to bring out all the self-righteousness in my nature. With all the services I went to I pretty soon knew everything by heart including many hymns. I could leave my mouth on automatic pilot and think of other things.

At this age I conceived the idea of becoming the first woman priest. I read up on all the arguments for and against having women playing a prominent role in the church. It was an idea that was to last for the next few years. I decided to study classics and religious knowledge for my A-levels when the time came. I was beginning to learn Latin and loved it. I felt sure I would also love Greek.

Chapter Nineteen: I Take up Nuisance Calls, Clerihews and Yoga

AT TWELVE or so, I started to make nuisance phone calls, aided and abetted by my friend Jennifer. Mindful of my father's phone bills I made them from Ealing Common Station having saved my pennies to do so. Jennifer and I would look through the phone book and select a victim. I did most of the talking. I usually put on what I thought was an adult voice. It may even have passed as such. While my voice was utterly undisguisable and recognisable to my friends, those who phoned us did sometimes mistake me for my mother. The usual form of my phone call was to offer my victims membership deals on various clubs like the FWA. Most of those I telephoned appeared to take me seriously until I told them the full title – the Fat Women's Association. If they were a pound or two overweight they probably assumed I knew them personally. Only one man I phoned on behalf of the SMC (Smelly Men's Co.) sussed me out before I got to the full explanation of the club's acronym. He put on the cunning tone of voice that I'd heard from the ladies at Child Guidance. I was on to him before he was on to me and told him I was called Mabel Lucie Atwell.

After a few weeks Jennifer and I tired of this game. I had done an occasional variant of providing a quick rhyme for some poor soul cursed with a surname like Smelly, which was more amusing, but more cruel.

While no one ever made me an obscene phone call as a kid, I was cursed with hundreds of them once I became a published writer. I was repaid with compound interest for those twenty or so calls from Ealing Common Station.

Apart from my instant rhymes for strangers I was beginning to make them up about the teachers. My mother was unwise enough to teach me about Clerihews. These were even easier than Limericks, in my opinion, because you didn't need the triple rhyme. Various teachers were given the Pitt-Kethley treatment. Unfortunately most of these rhymes were only passed on orally and not written down. About the only one that springs to mind was that about our poor harmless chemistry teacher:

Miss Baker
Was turned into a Quaker

When hit by a thunderbolt
Of about two thousand volt.
I was also rewriting various rhymes I'd heard from my parents. I'd been told the one which runs:
In days of old
When knights were bold
And paper was not invented,
Each wiped his arse
Upon the grass
And went away contented.
I solemnly worked my way through every other word for arse with appropriate rhymes. In one of the earliest, the knights "wiped their bums/ Upon their chums". In what was probably the funniest, "They wiped their sterns/ On ragged ferns." Again, my love for natural history was intruding. Only recently, a friend of my husband rang to tell me his most sensual experience was stripping off and shitting in a wood on a hot summer's day. I couldn't resist establishing what he'd wiped his bum with as my mind went back to "the knights of old". He'd used dock leaves apparently. Now why didn't I think of that?

In view of my easy capacity for light verse, it's a pity I didn't know about the *Spectator* and *New Statesman* competitions at that stage. Some praise or acceptance from the outside world might have mitigated the Hell of Haberdashers. I was not now being victimised by teachers, but I went my way doing the bare minimum of work in a mood of leaden acceptance. Occasionally I made stands on what I felt were points of principal. A couple of these involved joint projects, things I hated because my personality got submerged. In the first, under Miss Overton, I flatly refused to do one with the dunce of the form, an unhappy girl who got D for everything and spent most of her time scratching her legs. She didn't have eczema or anything that would give her a real need to scratch – she simply enjoyed the effect of seeing tiny pyramids of powdered skin on the floor. Miss Overton had only teamed us out of malice, of course. Left to my own devices I produced an interesting study of the Flora of Acton, complete with coloured ballpoint illustrations. In a later teaming, the following year under Miss Ashley, I was put with reasonably bright girls to make a board game of The Pilgrim's Progress. I did do slightly more of the work, but I still felt it was unfair that Miss Ashley wanted to send me alone to sign "The

Excellent Book" for this work. I insisted that the other two girls
went too. I discovered then that there's not a lot anyone can do,
when an individual digs her heels in.

In my pursuit of standing alone, or being able to do something
that others could not do, I taught myself Yoga long before it became
fashionable. My father had three books that had been sent to him
by a guru who wanted to be part of the ecumenical movement.
They were printed in India on thin paper, with murky photographs
of the man concerned bending himself into all sorts of positions. I
worked my way through all these, only drawing the line at swallow-
ing twenty-five yards of cloth to clean out my intestines. Most of the
rest was achievable with a little practice.

I do little Yoga now. I prefer the feel of faster more energetic
exercise. Yet, I believe the postures I learnt at twelve rendered me
permanently flexible. I can still fold myself into an unusual variety
of positions, something that has surprised and pleased many men
I've been to bed with. Though I've never done any ballet I am also
often mistaken for a dancer because of my ability to stretch out all
my body including the toes and ankles.

I liked the feel of the lotus. Haberdashers loved getting us to sit
cross-legged on the floor for prayers and assemblies. Here was a
chance to cross my legs the other way, with feet on top of genitals
rather than well hidden under my knees. It was a quiet act of insub-
ordination. I felt the sense that I was going "widdershins", a term
I'd come across only in fairy tales whose heroes occasionally went
anticlockwise round some stone or tree and then met an ogre. I had
been trying it for years, but the only ogres I met were teachers.

If I sat in the lotus position at assembly as an act of rebellion, it
was always a little awkward to get up because my feet had no con-
tact with the floor. I was still unknotting myself by the time others
were on their feet. I occasionally tried it in Gym lessons also. I even
balanced in this position, swinging between my hands, walking
around on them, or else combined it with a shoulder-stand. My
Gym teacher remained completely unimpressed by my antics. She'd
written me off as an unsporting so-and-so at the first glance. She
only had any liking for the most athletic two or three in any class.
As far as she was concerned, everyone else was a waste of time. It's
a pity when teachers of any subject have this attitude. Even the
worst pupils can make headway with a little individual help. Years

later I saw an old man who was rather senile draw women looking like tadpoles at an art class. The master took endless pains with him and within the year, the old man was beginning to see what was before him correctly. While he was never going to make a wonderful artist, he was at least drawing human bodies instead of tadpoles. I had respect for that teacher because of his patience with a pupil who was incredibly unpromising. If our gym teacher had believed that the other twenty or so pupils in her class had some possibilities we would have respected her more and learned more. As it was, we spent a lot of time making jokes about her being a lesbian. We had no actual proof that she was, only we reckoned that she liked looking at our tits a little too much. She used to sit in on school medicals. If the doctor thought we were round-shouldered or flat-footed she would prescribe exercises. Practically everyone was round-shouldered, because the sight of the gym teacher's burning eyes would make our chests cave in. None of us had the nerve to flaunt our tits in front of her.

The first school doctor had died about a week after saying I looked very unhealthy. We were on to our second doctor by now. For a dare, I asked: "Is it really necessary?" when I was asked to remove my bra in front of the gym teacher's burning eyes. Posture exercises were prescribed as I crumpled, faced with that intent stare. I was also given exercises for flat feet. I did these so religiously that I developed high insteps, which were a lot harder to find shoes for. I felt more comfortable clacking round in Scholls, but these were banned in school.

A year or two later our gym teacher got married. We all assumed that we had been wrong in thinking her a lesbian. We had never heard of bisexuals.

20: A Red Letter Day

I WAS STILL set in my rabidly pro-Celtic phase and had persuaded my mother to let us holiday twice in Ireland. The first time we went to the North via Liverpool. I had my one and only experience of seasickness on the Irish Sea. At least I think I did. To this day I've never quite been sure whether it was real sickness or the effect of eating a Cornish pasty washed down with bitter lemon. The next time I ate that particular brand of pasty I felt pretty much the same. A bitter lemon would probably have been the final straw.

It was just before the Troubles and Belfast was a safe enough place in those days. We stayed in a caravan in Groomsport, a tiny town by the sea. I loved the country and its greenness. We walked through leafy lanes full of wild fuschia to nearby Donaghadee. My mother was amused to see some "louts" as she termed them, watching me undressing behind my towel on the beach near there. They cheered as my knickers came off. Mum had an emerald green costume, a boned and zipped period piece from the Forties, elaborate as the top of an evening dress, but she had given up swimming. She believed, as do many women, that you have to be near perfect before you're allowed to expose yourself on beaches. I've never understood that point of view. Why shouldn't a woman be allowed to expose hairy legs, spots, cellulite, a monster bottom, etc? Not that I mean to suggest my mother had all of those faults. I can see a good case for giving the world a laugh if you can't dazzle it with your beauty. If I look like a McGill when I'm old, I'll still be going in the sea and hoping to entertain the great British public. When my knickers came off in front of the Irish boys, I kicked them off with a flourish. I'd learned that trick from my mother. She used to kick her knickers in the air and catch them to make my father laugh. But for her, comedy always had to be a private rather than a public matter.

I liked the ruggedness of the coastline, back in Groomsport. But everything was not quite what it seemed. I swam and got caught in thick seaweed. In another cove, I found what I took to be jewels, bright fragments of coloured glass that had been rounded off and smoothed by the action of the sea. I showed them to my mother who was equally impressed. When we got them back to the caravan in a blue plastic box that had held cheese spread, the stones had turned greyer and had scratched surfaces. I tried wetting them, but somehow they never looked as magical out of the sea.

While I loved the look of the country and the ability of the people to talk endlessly, even to a kid, I became conscious of another aspect that was less likeable. On the train to Belfast, on our homeward journey, I vividly described an Orange Day procession to some American tourists, telling them about what I thought was a very funny sight – men in bowler hats carrying drawn swords. My mother soon hushed me, becoming conscious of a most venomous glare from an Irish Protestant in the corner of the carriage.

The following year I went to Cork with Mum and again I was conscious of that same rigidity about religion. The caravan camp was two miles outside, so I walked into the town that weekend and spent hours looking around the highways and byways of Cork, getting to know every little street. It was Sunday and nearly time for evensong, so, when I'd got thoroughly lost I asked a woman to direct me to St. Ninian's which happened to be Protestant.

"I don't think that would be prudent!" she said and walked away. I found the cathedral by myself. I was totally charmed by Cork and enjoyed playing the bells of St. Ann's, which worked from a small keyboard. I also loved the river and all its bridges. My London upbringing had got me hooked on rivers. I still miss them, although I've grown to love the sea more.

There were all sorts of things I could have done but didn't because I was going through a period of not being able to get up in the morning. That phase lasted throughout my teens but vanished miraculously once I started doing paid work. Without the incentive of money I seemed to be unable to feel compos mentis before twelve. I often think I'd have been happier and more productive at school if I'd been paid to go there. Perhaps I should have been put to child labour instead.

Mum wanted to have a trip round a local brewery and a look at the local greyhound racing. I got up so late on the last Saturday that both trips were off. She always held it against me and brought up the subject from time to time for many years. I've never quite known what she intended to do at either venue as she didn't like beer, after her Plymouth Brethren upbringing, and she'd never placed a bet in her life.

One trip we did manage to make was to kiss the Blarney Stone, something that is supposed to give you the gift of the gab. I even have a certificate to prove it. Mum couldn't quite face hanging over the battlements to do it so she stayed down on ground level.

On one of my long walks round Cork I discovered a strange shop by the docks with a stuffed cow in the window – just that, no explanation even. My mother thought I was spinning a yarn until she saw it too on our way home. For years everyone I told the story to thought I was making it up, until I met a man from Cork who said that he knew the place well. The stuffed cow had belonged to a previous owner and had stayed there after the shop changed its use from taxidermy to taxis! I loved knowing the end of the story, the explanation. Whatever strange things we encounter in life, someone somewhere knows the reason behind, if only we have the fortune to meet that person.

In Groomsport I was a slightly plain child. My nose had grown to its present size and the rest of my face hadn't. By Cork I was beginning to have the seeds of adult looks. By applying thick make-up including the crude blue eye shadow, and putting my hair up I managed to pass for eighteen and get into *Up Pompeii* which had been given an X Certificate in Ireland. I travelled at half fare on the bus first, of course.

While I was still in love with Ireland I had my breasts, such as they were, felt by an Irish navvy in his hut round the corner from Creffield Road. He kept exhorting me to come back wearing a pair of stockings to see him. While I quite enjoyed the feeling of his hands on my breasts, I had enough sense not to go back, with or without stockings.

Before Christmas, on a Saturday when I was due to go to the Journalists' party with my father, my periods came on. I had been sitting by the fire in my parents' bedroom on a heap of papers brought back from Ireland. They were old-fashioned stories of doctor and nurse romances in cheap magazines with weak newsprint. I don't know quite why the papers had all been left lying there, months later. Perhaps some of them had been used to mop the handsome old shop clock, which lay by that fire and was now being used as a urinal by Messrs. Bunyan and Moriarty.

As I sat warming myself, conscious of a slight ache in my stomach, I noticed blood spreading on the papers below. By some bizarre coincidence I had managed to start my period all over *The Red Letter* and *The Red Star*. Mum soon produced one of her Dr.White's mouse's hammocks for me. I had a small black elastic sanitary belt in my dressing table in readiness.

I was pleased at first, until I realised what a bloody nuisance periods were. I had been jealous of the few girls who'd started them young. It seemed like membership of an exclusive club. By the end of that year, pretty well all the girls in the class were menstruating. When you had a period, the gym mistress allowed you to wear a pair of shorts as well as the regulation navy knickers in class. The old-fashioned sanitary towels were disgusting. If anyone didn't change them quite fast enough you could smell something vaguely kipper-like in the room. I always sensed that smell near the girls in grey shorts. It was not helped by the fact that our school had no showers nearby for us to use. I can still smell the combination of ropes, wood, foam mats, kippers and sweat that permeated the gym

Disposing of those massive towels was also a nuisance. Where there were no separate bins, and in private houses, you used to have to tear the thing to bits after you'd changed it. Bloody fragments would keep popping back up every time you flushed the loo. Then there was also a problem when the periods came on suddenly. For most of us, in the very early stages, they were highly irregular. It was only too easy for a spot of blood to come through on the back of your dress even if your knickers had caught most of the first gush.

By fourteen, I had become a firm devotee of tampons. My mother had some misgivings about this, as she'd never taken to them herself.

She kept saying: "You should have been around in my days when we had real towels to wash and put out on the line."

Perhaps my dildo experiment had made the first insertion a little easier, but I was happy with tampons immediately. I also firmly ignored all my mother's old wives' tales about swimming and washing my hair with periods and continued to do both without ill effects.

The one useful thing about a period was that you could use the faintest pain to get you out of class and into the sick room. It was an excuse that was always accepted in a girls' school. I don't suppose most of us did feel all that ill, but it was a chance to swing time off for an hour or two. As for pre-menstrual tension, none of us had even heard of it. I've never suffered it myself and I've met remarkably few women who have. Most of us are tense all the time.

Chapter Twenty-One: Holidaying Alone

AT THIRTEEN I began to conceive the urge to holiday alone. I'd had fantasies about going off and camping in a tent in the wilds with one or other friend. My mother handled this awful prospect in a very sensible way. She didn't absolutely veto it, but she got my Uncle Alex, who was at the time, a detective inspector in the CID in Swansea, to talk to me. He told me that they had instructions to pick up underage children when they were found camping in the wild. So that idea bit the dust. In about a year, I was to join the Youth Hostelling Association to do it all in a more legal way. I was able to cycle long distances by now and planned trips.

My first holiday away from parental supervision was with my friend Avril Jenkins at Canford Summer School of Music. Unfortunately her parents were there too, but it was still a taste of life away from home. At that age, Avril was fun, a bit like a girl from an Angela Brazil story. My mother had one or two old school annuals and somehow Avril reminded me of the girls of that era. She had a tough sporty manner and made jokes of a fairly innocuous kind about teachers. Miss Ashley loathed her on sight and did everything to needle her, something that upset me. Within a year or two I also began to like Avril less. She came from a strict Baptist family and started to tell one or two of us that we'd go to hell for drinking.

"Do you really think someone will go to hell for having a pint of lager?" I asked.

"No," she said. "But you will..."

At the time of my first trip to Canford we were firm friends. I had spent one night in Avril's house near Harrow. Her mother was the kind of woman who joins the WI and does classes in everything. She had no job, but every hour of her time was taken up with activities. She had taught Avril to be more or less self-sufficient so that she could have more time for all her hobbies. Avril usually made her own breakfast, unlike the rest of us.

On my over-night visit, Avril sneaked me by the back window of their bungalow in the evening, to see a bunch of middle-aged women standing around in corsets trying on clothes they had made. Most of the women, apart from Avril's mother, were seriously overweight and we thought the sight hilarious. Somehow none of them noticed us. They had not drawn the curtains because they thought they were unobserved. Mr. Jenkins was under strict orders not to traverse the garden at particular times.

Avril's family was musical. Both she and her mother played the cello. I believe the father played some other instrument, although I never found out what. Both the parents sang in choirs. Which was how we all ended up in Canford on the Bach course.

Avril's father was a PhD and always pushed her towards science subjects although she was reasonably all-round. She eventually became a haematologist. She had conceived this ambition fairly young. We were all going through a dirty stage and Avril was by far the least squeamish person amongst us. I had visions of her wiping bloody hands on a T-shirt in her future job.

Avril's father had promised to drive us to Dorset for the singing course, but there was a last-minute hitch and we went by train instead. My father let him insist on paying for my ticket. I wished he hadn't. When I got to Canford there was to be a further financial embarrassment. We had to buy music for the course and I didn't have enough money. My parents and I had no conception of the cost of sheet music and I'd only brought a small amount of pocket money. Avril's father bought her all the music and we shared. She sang alto and I was soprano, but we could manage by standing on the extreme edges of our sections. Fortunately I've always been able to hold a tune even with someone singing a different part on one side of me.

I loved singing all day and felt I was learning fast. Most of the course was Bach cantatas and I had to learn to pronounce the German words. There were one or two pieces in Latin too. While I was studying the classical version of the language, Church Latin was a novelty to me with its Italianate pronunciation. At that stage, sight-reading Bach was difficult for me, but I managed to muddle along. I felt I was being stretched and learning new things faster than I ever had at school. There were emotional highs to the music too. In the evenings there was a choral society where we sang Michael Tippett's Child of Our Time with a view to putting on a performance at the end of the week.

Essentially everything at Canford was aimed at putting on scratch performances in concerts at the end of the week. The standard was a great deal better than the average local scratch Messiah. All the participants were genuinely musical and many were professionals taking a busman's holiday. There was a full orchestra for everything and professional soloists. Every year a man would bring a couple of harpsichords he'd made in the back of his van. I was highly amused by this at the time. When I became friendly with the writer Michael Bywater I realised that this was part of the course for lovers of Baroque instruments. He plays harpsichords with names like Tracy and talks with enthusiasm of the mad world of the keyboard player.

For the next few years I went back to Canford, usually on my own, though Avril turned up a couple of years later. I got music from my local library to cut down on the expense of buying copies. It meant I could run through things first too, without the need to sight-read everything. The following year we sang Bach's B-Minor Mass and it became one of my favourite pieces of music – one I'd definitely take to a desert island. There were other ambitious projects in later years – Stravinsky's Les Noces, or Berlioz's Requiem performed in a local church. I sat too near the timpani for that and went slightly deaf for a week.

By contrast my school music lessons rarely introduced me to anything good. We mostly sang English folk songs in unison, or were taught trendier numbers like Kum-by-ya by a young music teacher who played the guitar. In a sense our teachers were pessimists. They made the assumption that we would be bored by anything good. Sometimes that was the case. Miss Watts, the Head of Music, once played us some Wagner and I was the only one who liked it. But perhaps Wagner was far from being the ideal choice in a school that was probably about twenty per cent Jewish. I remember there being many girls like Avril who played an instrument and sang tolerably, but somehow our needs for listening to or singing good music were not met. In the sixth I became friendly with Hannah Cole, one of the most musical girls. Her father was a composer and music critic for the Guardian. I only grew to like her towards the end of school when we studied Classics together and sometimes talked about opera. I had assumed she was a prig because she never broke the rules and was always held up as a model to the rest of us – something that does not endear a girl to her fellow pupils. Her mother was a former pupil of Haberdashers', which may have had something to do with teachers singling her out.

Apart from all the singing at Canford, there was good scratch instrumental music. One of the Canford traditions was to play the whole of the Brandenburg Concertos on the last night, going on into the small hours. After that there was a party where various classical musicians tried their hand at jazz. I drank some highly alcoholic punch there. Fortunately the senior Jenkinses had gone to bed and Avril didn't tell tales. I didn't get drunk then and managed miraculously to avoid doing so until my late teens when it was legal.

In that first year, I hoped for an adventure of some kind. In the middle of the week there was a dance. I rather fancied the first boy I danced with. He was a sixth former from Canford School, doing a summer job waiting at tables at the course. On learning my age, he soon defected to an older girl. The age gap between the men I fancied and myself was to be a constant problem at this time. When they learned how young I was and vanished, I took it personally. I saw it as some failure in myself. How I wish, looking back on things, that someone had explained to me that no decent man takes up with an under-age girl and that my best hope of something approaching a relationship was picking a boy who was under-age too.

I had begun going to youth clubs and had one date at this stage. He was someone I picked up at the end of a youth club disco. We went to an X film to see his favourite star, Carol White. He drooled over her and didn't lay a finger on me. It was a fine summer evening, but he brought a huge city gent's umbrella with him, a fact that made him look decidedly more peculiar than he had at the disco. Neither of us had the faintest inclination to make a second date. To this day I can't remember his name, although I suppose he must have had one.

I went to two youth clubs. One was at St. Martin's and the other at St. Matthew's in Ealing. St. Martin's drew the rougher kids. Sometimes we held séances with me as the medium. The girls usually asked questions like what colour knickers they were wearing. Somehow I always got these questions right.

I enjoyed talking with girls who were working begging scams. One made quite a nice little income from asking for change to use in the telephone. Endless men would give her a few pence rather than change half a crown. In an hour it could amount to pounds. Then she'd move on to another telephone box. I also learned how to play darts, after a fashion.

I was getting very dress-conscious and Mum encouraged this, even going to the lengths of making me a short transparent pink silk chiffon dress when I dreamed up the idea. Neither she nor my father seemed to mind me going round looking like jailbait.

Oddly, it was not when I was dressed up to the nines that I got most offers. There were endless kerb-crawlers along the stretch of the Uxbridge Road that ran by the common up to Ealing Broadway. Invariably, when these men stopped to offer me a lift or proposition me, I was in school uniform and not made-up or dressed to look older than my real age. Most of the middle-aged men who propositioned schoolgirls offered ten bob. It was not a particularly generous offer, even for those days. Yet, I suppose it might well have appealed to the seven-year-old cocksucker from Springfield Gardens, or the girl who worked a scam outside telephone booths. I suppose also that anyone who had pocketed all those ten bobs and invested them in shares might be a very rich woman today.

Chapter Twenty-Two: The Rogue Molecule

AT FOURTEEN I started learning Greek and loved it. I picked up the alphabet in a day and taught my mother so that we could use it as a code. There had been a choice between learning German and Greek. I wanted to learn both, but figured I'd never be able to teach myself Greek. I've had various tries at learning German since, but never progressed far, because of laziness. I think my decision was right though. I wish that the Classics were part of most children's learning. Occasionally journalists have consulted me for a quote on this matter and been surprised by my answer. They had assumed that someone who swears like a trooper wouldn't want Latin taught in schools. They obviously don't realise that the best tradition in obscene satirical verse lies in Latin and Greek literature and that it's this tradition I have attached myself to rather than modern performance verse. When I compiled *The Literary Companion to Sex* one or two ignorant reviewers even accused me of putting rude words into poets like Martial!

My first couple of years of Latin had been with a jolly teacher, Mrs. Wood. She allowed a certain amount of misbehaviour. The only thing she really disapproved of was chewing gum. Occasionally we'd all pretend to have a mouthful of the stuff, circling our jaws like a herd of cows. At other times we'd plant a tiny piece of it in the flowers on her desk. She'd complain that she smelt some gum in the room but was never able to locate it. After Mrs. Wood, for the two years leading to O level another teacher taught us. She was prim and slightly sour but reasonably fair. We nicknamed her *Pompey* because she resembled him strongly, if you can imagine him with a perm and a pair of thick glasses. She was firm friends with the other Latin and Greek teacher who was known as *Phoebe* because she looked vague and it seemed to fit her. *Phoebe* was horribly thin and rode a bike. She looked awfully like her bike except that she wore long Gor-ray skirts and tiny jumpers from the Thirties. She was known for being excessively mean with her portions at lunchtime. We would groan if we saw her at the head of the table, knowing that we'd be fed like Oliver Twist while she heaped the remainder on her own plate. We theorised that all her clothes were saved from her youth and that she lived on that one large meal a day. Further evidence of her meanness was evinced in the way she'd use a piece of chalk until the last quarter of an inch, scraping her fingernails on the board. I can still cringe even thinking of that noise. Her tiny Thirties jumpers all had short sleeves and she would wipe the board with her lower arms and hands. Her knuckles were always red and raw from cycling in all weathers without gloves. I can still see the powdered chalk on red raw skin.

Phoebe always seemed slightly frightened of me. Her English was poor and ungrammatical so she would always correct my translations to include a wrong preposition with a verb. It was odd that someone could come through a Classical education and yet manage to have slightly bad grammar. She was a northerner of some kind. We never quite tracked down the accent; the nearest I heard to it was Davenport's. Perhaps she was used to a different set of idioms. I can't think of any other explanation. *Phoebe* was also very prim sexually. She took about five minutes to translate some Greek phrase for rape in a passage from Homer. She coloured red as a radish and came out with something like "made love secretly by force".

Phoebe and *Pompey* were firm friends and shared a kind of snobbishness. *Pompey* was even worse in this respect. She took a few other students and myself to a classical symposium. On the way we had to make light conversation with her. Light conversation consisted of her telling us what newspapers we should be reading then asking us, one by one, which we read. By the time I got to my turn, I realised that a) I couldn't be bothered to read them myself and preferred a good book, and b) my parents took the one she had just slated as lacking in intellectual content, *The Daily Telegraph*. I lied and said we took the *Times* and gained a grudging approval. Looking back on it I wish I'd fulfilled her worst expectations by saying *The News of the World*.

At that time there were three of us in the Greek class. My co-pupils were Juliet who ended up in Norway married to a farmer, and Barbara Levy who went on to become a literary agent. Both were undoubtedly swots while I was not. I consistently got worse marks, yet had more of a feel for the literature and the mythology. I think Juliet and Barbara always saw the subject as one that could be learned meticulously in order to get good results in exams. There was no real love for it in either of them.

About the same time I started learning Greek I also took up snogging. My introduction came at a friend's parties. She was a doctor's daughter whose parents took an urbane view of her sexual activities. She boasted that her mother put the Pill on her porridge every morning. Contrary to all the popular myths about sex and academic achievement not going together, she combined an active sex life with excellent exam results, and went on to get a good degree from Oxford, married young and became a lawyer. She also had the knack of eating like a horse and staying exceedingly slim. Some people would like to think she will pay for it all in the next incarnation. My view is that her success came from a remarkable quality of directness. While most girls displayed a lot of false modesty and wouldn't really state their aims, she was prepared to say "I want that and I'm going to have it" about everything from a couple of extra cream cakes to men, a degree and marriage.

She knew a wide circle of boys from St. Paul's. When her parents were away we'd all party. Her parents didn't seem to mind what happened as long as the house was cleaned afterwards.

I was still in my religious phase so I stopped earlier than my hostess. At one of those parties I remember French kissing two boys, one after the other, then freezing in their arms. It was the only way I could stop myself going further.

I had not been sure I would enjoy a French kiss. One of the Pinner Set had tried to describe it for us, years before. In her version the man's tongue went "right down the throat" which just sounded uncomfortable. Then and now, I was conscious of how most people describe sexual activities of all kinds inaccurately. If only they looked at their own bodies realistically, they would not get things so wrong. If the girl from Pinner had stuck her tongue out in front of a mirror she would have seen that the organ concerned is far too short to go down throats.

In time I was to gain a better grasp on reality by drawing the human form. Those who learn anything about anatomy, whether it is from the artistic, athletic or medical point of view, don't suffer from an unreal perception of the body's actions in the way that the rest of the world does.

While my perceptions were more accurate than the Pinner girl's I wasn't experiencing what women are supposed to experience – sex and love in the same package. Perhaps the two things go together far less than the media would have us believe. Perhaps many women as well as men experience them separately more often than together.

Sex, attraction, friendship and a relationship weren't to come together in my life until my late thirties. My experiences with the dildo happened with a girl I didn't either fancy or like. My snogging with boys went with attraction only; there was no relationship. In the same year I went in for breast feeling sessions with two of my girl friends. Again I was not in love with them. I simply liked the sensation and also the opportunity to look at different shapes of breasts. In the next few years I was attracted to several men but had no relationship with them. I went out with a few I didn't particularly like or fancy and nothing happened. I snogged a few more boys at parties or on holidays, simply because I enjoyed the sensation in the same sort of way that I enjoyed having my breasts felt by a girl. Doing something to alleviate boredom was a major motive in most of these situations. As an adult, I was more likely to leave and have sex with a stranger after a bad party than a good one. For many years, after school, most of my affairs were based on attraction and the need to alleviate boredom until I met the man I married.

Not everyone followed my path or that of my friend, the party-giver. Some of the other girls were more cautious. Juliet, who was in my Greek class, lectured me on how to keep a man's respect after seeing me snogging. I still fail to understand her attitude and that of women like her. Only my religion stopped me from going further, without that I'd have gone all the way immediately. I couldn't bear the idea of restraining the expression of feelings in order to dangle a man. I've never wanted to do that. I didn't keep those boys by freezing and going no further. I didn't want to. If a man is kept by being led on then slapped down, there are no real strong bonds in the relationship. Another woman could do the same at any time. The whole situation is doomed to failure.

I thoroughly enjoyed my first experience of French kissing. Mum had told me it was disgusting and unfanciable which made me begin to doubt her tastes and her sanity once I'd tried it. She has subsequently told me that she only said that to keep me out of trouble. I don't agree with that form of tuition. It is all part of the lying process, like Juliet's theories on handling men.

We were taught Science in a not dissimilar way. One year we were told that everything dropped at 32 feet per second. The intelligent amongst us asked questions like: "What about a feather?" We were hushed up till the following year when it was deemed we were old enough to learn that the rate things fell at was dependent on their density. The teachers concerned fell in my estimation faster than any feather. I quit Physics as soon as I could. If we were to be told a "truth" one year, only to have it changed the next, I couldn't believe in the subject any more.

There are many other ways in which Science is wrongly and unattractively taught in schools. If we'd been introduced to the personalities of great scientists of the past as well as their theories the whole subject could have been more interesting. In English and Art we learn about the creators of various works, why not in Science? I read up on some great scientists of the past when I was studying the Occult in my late teens. In a funny sort of way the subject's related. The experimental scientist was often outlawed by the Church, together with the witch. If only our teachers had introduced us to these heroes and their writings the whole subject would have been a lot more colourful. Instead of Newton and his beautiful clear prose, all we got was a wrong theory of gravity, followed by a better one when we were thought the right age to learn it.

I quite enjoyed Chemistry in the early stages. The paraphernalia had a certain beauty – bright blue copper sulphate crystals, strangely shaped glass vessels and the chance to play with fire legally. I even had a set at home to play with, making soap, etc. It was fun, but something I didn't believe in. I felt there was a flaw in Chemistry's logic long before I'd heard of empirical reasoning. If a thousand experiments went one way, to me it was no proof that the next wouldn't go another. I put it to my teacher that molecules might have souls or minds and that, somewhere, every million or so, there would be an exceptional one that thought differently from the rest and went its own way. I was obviously made for the Arts rather than Science. As far as Haberdashers' was concerned I was definitely the rogue molecule.

Chapter Twenty-Three: I Give Up English

AT ABOUT THIS period a new and attractive History teacher entered our lives – Miss Baillie-Reynolds. She was tall and handsome in a slightly masculine way. More importantly she appeared to talk to us as equals and described history in dashing colloquial language. Almost the whole class fell in love with her. I even managed to find an Edwardian novel by someone from her family. I assumed this would please her, but my form mistress, Mrs. Dorling, who had never been an admirer of mine, told me off for my pains. My action was supposed to be "impertinent". I can't think why. Personally I'd be pleased if someone showed me a book by my grandfather.

Of course, Mrs. Dorling simply enjoyed any opportunity to tell me off. Scots usually have strong feelings about me, one way or the other, and she was one of those who disliked me on sight. She taught the top division of the Maths class. I deliberately flunked one exercise and turned in some grubby graphs in order to get moved down a division so that I could be in with one of our most likeable teachers. Mrs. Berry was probably the nicest-natured mistress of the lot. She always showed patience to both the bright and the dull and always took time explaining everything. We never saw her get angry with anyone. Her humane system seemed to work and there was never any disorder in her classes. Perhaps the fact that she had a deaf daughter had given her this patience with other children.

Not deterred by Mrs. Dorling's telling-off I started the Baillie-Reynolds Association. Inspired by its acronym we took the paper napkin our heroine had used at lunch, divided it into a dozen or more portions for members of the society, and wore it in our bras. Our hearts beat faster for a while.

Eventually, one of the class filled in a form for her to receive free condoms. Our teacher took this gesture of our affection with so little humour that we fell out of love with her immediately. A handwriting expert was called in to examine samples of everyone's writing in the class. I don't know what he made of all the books in our desks. We used to alleviate the boredom of class by reading copies of *The Perfumed Garden* and other sex classics during lessons. Some of the doctors' daughters obtained some really interesting manuals from their father's surgeries. I borrowed one on lesbians from my friend Annette, who was half-Swedish. When she found I'd taken it home and let Mum read it too, she was too terrified to visit my house any longer. She even doubled up and walked like Groucho Marx when passing our privet hedge. She little realised that my mother had simply read the book with interest and had no intention whatsoever of punishing its lender.

Poor Lucinda got the blame for the condom incident. The condom form had been filled in by a left-handed writer, which meant that my mother's and my handwriting never even came under suspicion. Lucinda got the full lecture although she was, for once, innocent. I eventually found out who had done it – one of the good girls, a swot who never misbehaved in class and who, consequently, never even came under suspicion.

We had a new headmistress now, Miss Gillette. Old Harry and her girlfriend had retired and were to die within a few years. It was a curious tendency – few of my teachers were able to survive retirement, often dying in their early sixties. Only the youngest ones are still alive.

Miss Gillette told Lucinda that she had "no moral fibres" – at least that was how we heard it reported afterwards. It was hinted at this stage that neither of us was a good influence on the other and that we probably should not be friends. Of course we ignored that completely.

Lucinda, unlike me, was mad on Pop. She would persuade me to buy some awful bubble gum so that she could have the pictures of the Beatles that went with it. She also persuaded me to join the Beatles Fan Club. While I've never been a fan of theirs, I do consider that their songs are the bearable end of that kind of music. If anyone asked me what I liked at the youth club, it was safest to say one of their records, on the grounds that I could stand listening to something like: "Hey Jude" without feeling physically ill. Any Pop with a heavy electronic beat almost disables me, to this day. I have some kind of aural sensitivity induced by bad music, particularly when it's loud, that can make me physically retch and be in pain for hours afterwards.

The one thing I did like about joining the Beatles Fan Club was the chance to write to boys from countries all over the world. These correspondences usually fizzled after a letter or two. I even suggested in front of Phoebe that both I and the rest of the class should try to find some Greek boys to correspond with via this club to improve our writing of the language. She looked at me as if I was a turd on her boot, or a skunk at a picnic. Barbara Levy, I think, might have been up for it though, if we had not both been persuaded by Phoebe that modern Greek bore so little resemblance to the old version that there was no point.

Lucinda was also corresponding with boys. She even answered an advert from a dubious character in *Time Out* and received a nine-page pencilled letter of his desires. The letter was circulated amongst us like copies of *The Perfumed Garden*. The writer was not entirely literate but he knew what he wanted and boasted that it would all be safe because he had "draws full of rubber goods".

At this stage we were all busy looking for erotic material. For a horrible joke I tricked a friend called Freda into reading a very boring Victorian novel called *Cobwebs and Chains*. I never actually told her there was anything in it. I just sat there with it, licking my lips, then refused to tell her what it was about. That was enough to get her going, though she cursed me afterwards. On another occasion, Margaret Francocci, a half-Italian half-Irish girl with a large bosom, got a whole party of us to listen while she read a scene she considered "dirty". We lurked around her up by the potting shed. While we listened, Mary, one of the Pinner Set, put the school guinea pig down her own blouse. It burrowed into one of her sleeves and crapped unnoticed on her inner elbow as we listened to the so-called erotica. The scene turned out to be from one of the James Bond books, a bit where 007 is tied to one of his girls and lowered to the sharks. It was not what Margaret had led us to believe. Come to think of it, half the sex books were disappointing in other ways. I'm glad I read them early though. It cut down the time needed for research when I came to edit *The Literary Companion to Sex*.

I decided to drop what would have been my ninth O-level subject, History, at this stage. Miss Baillie-Reynolds, our former heroine, had decided we should study the Nineteenth century. My tastes had always been for earlier times. I discovered archaeology at this period and started going on digs. My first was in Elstow, John Bunyan's hometown. I had always been an admirer of John Bunyan's simple vivid English and was glad to see the place he came from. Our dig was on an earlier monastery site and we stayed in nearby Bedford. I went with Jennifer and Felicity, who regularly accompanied me on various cycling and youth hostelling trips.

My first trip with Jennifer and Felicity had been to Oxford. I decided to cycle all the way. They were meeting me there, starting only from Aylesbury. I must have been cycling in a dream because I managed to go on to the M40 with the general stream of traffic. I soon realised I wasn't welcome by the beeping of the cars and climbed over the side and down a grassy bank to rejoin quieter roads. I told the incident to one or two friends after and it came back to me in wonderfully exaggerated forms. Very soon I was cycling down the M1 wearing my see-through pink chiffon.

For our archaeological week in Elstow we did it the easy way and took the train. We figured that archaeology would be far too hard work to be combined with cycling. We were right about that. I found myself learning to use a pick at the tender age of fourteen. I swung it with force and venom, so much so that the director of the dig soon realised I might do someone a mischief and put me on more delicate jobs like scraping away with a trowel or cleaning bones with a toothbrush.

While I was involved in the latter activity, one of the boys stole my pink rubber gloves and blew them up. They looked so remarkably like udders that he proceeded to milk them with accompanying noises in front of the rest of the dig. I can't remember his name if I ever knew it, but I can still remember the way that he kept us entertained with that joke and another which involved imitating a donkey in heat in order to draw a real-life donkey from the next field. Like many of the teenagers who go on digs he was also studying Classics, although I suppose he might have come from a farming background to be able to reproduce those noises so faithfully.

We all used the local pub and ate hearty ploughman's lunches washed down with lager. In the next few years I was only refused entry to a pub once, when I went with a friend who was actually of the right age, but who looked younger.

I went on a further dig in Bedford itself, that summer, and the following year in Cardiff, after I'd done my O-levels. I got the results while I was still there. I passed all eight with middling grades except for an A in art.

O-levels had been one set of exams that we could not cheat on. The desks were too far apart and the whole thing was properly invigilated. There was none of our usual business of writing answers on blotting paper and holding them up, or carrying scraps of vital information in our pockets. I had one horrendous day in my exams when I had to sit three papers – a total of eight hours – in one day. The other Greek students had sat their French in the Spring, by not doing this the times of my exams overlapped and I had to sit them one after the other with a teacher guarding me over lunch and when I went to the lavatory. The cook had to give me lunch at a different time. She poured extra food on to my plate in sympathy – a pity because I hated macaroni cheese. Miss Lane who was set to guard me had even offered me a night in her house so that I could sit one paper the next day, but I refused. She was one teacher who genuinely liked me. She had a broad Lanarkshire accent. Most of us used to imitate it behind her back. I never understood why she liked me, because I gave up her subject, Geography, as soon as I possibly could.

The Cardiff dig was even more fun than the Elstow one. I have always enjoyed the literal act of digging, something few people understand. I find, even now, that an hour or two's digging down my allotment enhances the problem-solving part of my brain. I can then go in and write the awkward end of a chapter or resolve the end of a poem.

The first three days in Cardiff it rained as it can only rain in Wales. We did little but cart buckets of mud out of the trenches to try to save what had already been done. A local farmer rented a pump to the dig and it sucked out water noisily all day, but we could still hardly keep up with the rain. The dig was out in the countryside on what had once been a Roman farm. At one stage I almost thought I'd found something valuable, but it turned out to be a ring off a tractor rather than Roman or Celtic jewellery.

My life on the dig was a pattern of over-eating and heavy manual work. It's the pattern I feel healthiest on. All the food gives me energy and the exercise stops it putting on weight. Even now I seem to need to break up my writing day with a lot of physical activity. In between meals on the dig I ate vast quantities of bara brith, a heavy Welsh fruit bread, plastered with butter. I can recollect having nine slices one after the other as a snack. The previous year I had bought my mother Rabelais's Works for Mother's Day. Presumably I sympathised with gargantuan appetites of all kinds.

In the evening, we played Bridge or Chess or got off with one another. We wondered if one of the girls was bonking the middle-aged director. Her clothes at night were even more blatant than my pink chiffon. She frequently put on a pair of hand-crocheted bell-bottom trousers with no knickers underneath. Her mousy pubic hair poked through the stitches quite visibly.

At that stage I played what I think of as my last game of chess with one of the boys. Although I had liked the game very much when I first learned it, in a girls' school I had found no one to play with. I taught one or two and they were even worse than I was. It took playing a boy, someone who had not been taught by myself, to realise I wasn't much good at the game. If I had realised as a child what I know now, I would probably have worked hard at it and joined chess clubs and gone in for tournaments. I have always been able to channel my intelligence and become good at anything I really want to become good at. Chess is a game where there are some intelligent and interesting men and only a minute percentage of women. At the last tournament I viewed there was only one woman player amongst sixty men.

My last game at Cardiff at the age of fifteen and a half was with a boy who fancied me but whom I didn't fancy. Instead I snogged secretly with a rather short but amusing Scotsman. Looking back on it, I don't think I was the only string to Lennie's bow. Probably one or two others also got to lie on his bed and have "Can I undo your bra?" whispered in their ear in strong Glaswegian.

At the end of the dig my O-level results came in. I was happy enough that I'd passed all with middling grades apart from the A in Art. I knew I never did my best in exams and that was all I had hoped for. When I returned to school in the autumn I would be starting to study for four A-levels – Latin, Greek, Religious Knowledge and Art. Some people showed surprise I was not going to take English any further. I dropped it the minute I could. I had always loathed the subject and didn't particularly take to its teachers. If they were not psychotic like Miss Ashley, they lived in some impotent fantasy world where they thought about becoming writers but never actually did anything about it, like "Eggy" Everett. After her, I had two more dislikeable ones. First there was Miss Daines, known as "Lazy Daisy", who could hardly ever be bothered to mark anyone's work and spoke in class as if everything was too much effort. She never had a kind word to say about anything I wrote. I can still remember her reducing my whole report mark by giving me a C+ for a term's English. I pointed out to my mother that my two individual marks in the term had been A and B+. For once Mum did make a fuss. How could these have been averaged down to C+, she wanted to know. Miss Daines replied: "Her class work isn't much good!" The same could have been said of her.

It's funny how, even years later, we all resent the petty injustices heaped on us by teachers. I got together with Felicity and Jennifer a few years ago and they were still full of resentment. I had lost some of mine, because I'd turned some of the incidents into poems and so profited from them.

After Miss Daines came Miss Mowat. She was certainly a more active teacher, but she suffered from a kind of pretension that made her a laughing-stock. Her inner fantasies were obviously about the modelling world rather than writing. She was six foot tall with badly dyed red hair. She had taught herself to walk hips first like the old-fashioned type of catwalk model. Her legs and hips clad in a tweed tunic would enter the room long before the rest of her. We imitated her endlessly behind her back.

Our O-level books had been Jane Eyre, Romeo and Juliet and a selection of Keats. Miss Mowat wallowed in romance whether it was St. Agnes' Eve, star-crossed lovers, or the eventual triumph of a plain governess. Jane Eyre is, of course, a heroine that many teachers choose to identify with. Naturally I couldn't resist writing a St. Agnes' Eve version about our teacher and some particularly hideous lover mingling with her dreams. As a teacher she laid herself open to this sort of thing. There was a kind of hubris in her methods that brought on Nemesis. She was in the habit of reading out the odd passage from essays and mocking them publicly. Those who had contempt poured on their similes never forgave her. She didn't try this particular treatment on me, but she did christen me "Grace Poole" when we were at the stage of the book when those who had not read it before assumed that Grace was the lunatic in the attic. There was a kind of playing to the gallery in all these attempts, but it failed miserably. Even the less universally popular girls each had their own small group of friends who resented her sneers on their behalf. And so Miss Mowat, more than most of our teachers, became the butt of constant jokes behind her back.

At the final parents' meeting in that year, she told my mother. "Fiona's work's not all that good and she'll have to do Chaucer next year." My mother was able to reply with pride: "She's already read

the whole of Chaucer and she doesn't want to study English any
longer!"

Chapter Twenty-Four: A Midsummer Night's Dream

AFTER O-LEVELS I began to play truant. The term petered out with a series of lectures and it was easy to bunk off. I spent my time on these occasions reading Elizabethan and Jacobean plays. I managed to work my way through most of the minor ones, getting them either from school or on the library inter-loan. I also avidly read Mediaeval Poetry. I wished I had managed to play truant years before. It seemed like a chance to learn something.

I only attended the lectures I thought might be interesting. I turned up for an American astronaut. He was so phenomenally dull, I can't even remember his name. Obviously he had left his mind behind in space. I also attended the VD lecture where one of the older girls shocked teachers by asking if condoms helped prevent disease. The lecture was definitely not hard core as it was given by a nun.

In the following term, our uniform for the Sixth consisted of a grey skirt and turquoise blouse rather than the decidedly old-fashioned bottle green tunics we'd worn for years. We were all measured by a woman tailor who called out our sizes aloud. I opted for a second-hand skirt after being measured. They were so basic in shape there wasn't much point in having them tailor-made expensively. As term wore on we all turned our hems up higher and higher. Occasionally we were caught and reprimanded. There was a school rule about having them only four inches above the floor when we knelt. Haberdashers' always liked to see us kneeling.

Juliet had given up Greek and there were only two of us in the class, yet a third teacher of the subject was provided. Mrs. Zvegintzov was a great improvement on the others. When we first met she said that certain other teachers had told her all about me, but that she was prepared to make up her own mind.

Mrs. Z, as we called her, was an excellent teacher although she sometimes expected too much of others. An older girl from Haberdashers told me that she'd been told airily to read half the Iliad in Greek over the weekend. Of course, it would have been nothing to Mrs. Z, but somehow the way Classics was taught had not instilled any belief in us that we could romp through great books just for pleasure. Phoebe, especially, had always required us to have cribs at hand and take our dose of literature in extremely small bites. I wished that I had only been taught by Mrs. Z from the beginning. I also wished that I had learned Greek and Latin much younger, when my memory was perfect between the ages of six and eight. I'm inclined to think that you only have a hope of being really good at languages if you start young. Most of the best linguists I know were brought up bilingual and those I meet who speak English well in countries like Greece, Israel or Egypt, have generally started learning it almost as soon as they started going to school. Our system of leaving it all to the secondary stage is not a good one. It's probably responsible for the fact that most of the English cannot speak any other languages well.

In the first year of the sixth form a local boys' school put in a request for several girls to act in a production of a Midsummer Night's Dream. Miss Gillette decided to allow it, as we didn't have any important exams that year. About ten or so of us decided to audition and trouped over to Ealing Boys' Grammar School. The English master was a genial and eccentric man. He heard us read and then the female drama teacher got us to do some movement with her. She demanded that we remove our shoes, a request that embarrassed most of us as several of us had toes hanging out of the feet of our tights.

The English master proved to be splendidly eccentric. I was invited to tea in his house in Wembley at a later date. A whole wall of one room was taken up with painted papier maché codpieces he'd made specially for the play. They were all extremely large and had grotesque gilded faces.

I got Titania's part. I suppose at the time I would have preferred the idea of playing Hermia or Helena, but looking back, I believe the fairy kingdom suited my nature better. I've always taken the view that fairies were earthy outsiders who lived outside normal society and did everything their way. I've never seen them as sylphs with ballet skills. Playing Titania also gave me a chance to sing at the end.

The English master had wanted to have the fairies appearing naked, but the school governors wouldn't wear it. Instead the youngest got tie-dyed tights and leotards in camouflage colours. Oberon and Titania were to wear gold and silver lamé cat suits. These were so indecent that we needed another set of tights under them. They were also perilously fragile. The little boys delighted in filling my bower with pins until my suit was laddered into a state of indecency. Titania's part is quite a trial to any actress, because it involves lying asleep for half an hour or so on stage. When your bed is as full of pins as a Fakir's it can be sheer torture.

I did not get on particularly well with the boy who played Bottom, which enabled me to be extra, realistic when the magic spell wore off and I told Oberon how much I loathed the ass before me. The school had hired a wonderful Ass' head from a theatrical company. The only trouble was that it was extremely heavy. As Ralph who played Bottom turned to rest this head on me it would land on my diaphragm with a huge wallop, knocking the air out of me. Like a true professional I stifled all noises of pain from this and the pins. The show must go on, I thought. A few years later Bottom went on to become a town-councillor in Ealing, which seemed singularly appropriate.

Our version had moments of high comedy too. It was the season for colds and sore throats and Puck came armed with a tin of Strepsils. While on stage in half-naked state, he kept these down his large codpiece. There were curious clunks and rattles every time he did a cartwheel on stage.

Haberdashers' had not allowed us any time off homework during the play. I can still remember sitting in the silver cat suit translating Xenophon before I went on stage. I knew I would be too tired afterwards, besides the make-up took so long to clean off. My face and hands were painted silver. No cleanser seemed able to shift it all. I remember still seeing metallic traces in my bath water, weeks later.

I made friends with several boys but did not develop relationships with them. Instead I fantasised about their married music master. For a while I stayed friends with Lawrence Mynott and Stephen Calloway, who were both involved in the design of the play. Stephen went on to become the curator of the V and A, and Lawrence is still an artist. I even once came on a cartoon he had done of me for the Observer. Lawrence went to the same Art School as myself, later.

Two of Mrs. Judd's set of girls played Hermia and Helena. Belinda Crawford and Annette Haynes had both taken Speech lessons for years. I often wonder why Belinda did not take up acting professionally. She was also one of the prettiest girls in the year. I suppose someone somewhere had told her it was not a safe career. When I was thirty or so, I heard Belinda had ended up with a well-paid managerial job in the retail trade. It was probably safer, but I have to believe it was a lot more boring than becoming an actress.

Most of the Haberdashers' girls were not risk-takers by nature. The dream our teachers were selling us day by day was essentially a small suburban one. We were to get good exam results in academic subjects and then go on to university, preferably Oxford or Cambridge. The Haberdashers' dream didn't seem to stretch beyond degree level. There was almost no career advice on offer. By my last year a Careers mistress was appointed, but we sensed she had little experience. It was only a part time job on the side of her other teaching. The most anyone could get from her would be an idea which subjects they should take at university for a particular career. At a parents' meeting while we were still in primary school, our mothers and fathers were also sold the idea that we'd almost all get married early as well as having careers. My mother says she heard the parents breathe an audible sigh of relief.

Haberdashers' was certainly wrong about the marriage dream. I went to a large Old Girls' reunion, twelve or thirteen years after school. Jane Werenick who studied Art with me and went on to become an engineer, had the idea that we should all get together when we were thirty. Those who didn't turn up all had friends who did and who could report on them. The general impression I got was that half had not married and only a small percentage had children. Perhaps that's a pattern amongst educated women these days. I remember one of my friends saying: "It was either a child or a mortgage. I preferred the mortgage. I certainly couldn't have managed both." Perhaps we were simply late starters. Who knows what the picture would be if we all met up together again at forty, fifty, sixty and so on. No such reunions are planned.

I haven't met enough of the Haberdashers' girls in recent years to know if they were pleased with the way the school dream turned out. I would hazard a guess that at least some of them are discontent with their lot. I've met many people from all walks of life who have deeply regretted not taking a chance whether it was for acting, art, music or creative writing. Unless you have a private income the prospect of years of struggle and uncertainty is daunting. Yet, I would encourage everyone who might regret not doing so in the years to come, to take that leap of faith.

From the Haberdashers' point of view girls were told to keep away from the Arts as anything but a polite recreational hobby. I was continually encouraged to give up my fourth A-level, Art. It was not an academic subject. It wouldn't count in the eyes of the world, I was told. In the end, it was this attitude more than anything else that caused me to rebel.

Ealing Grammar School gave me a taste of acting Shakespeare in a mixed company and I loved every minute of it. I had always loved reading and acting Shakespeare's plays, yet continually I had been cast as a man in my school. I had read aloud all the best men's parts in class. In the costumed plays and playlets put together by teachers and girls I had started with the Dragon against St. George, followed by the Red Death, Shylock, Malvolio and Doctor Chasuble. Those parts mirrored the image my school had of me – diabolical at ten, a virus at eleven, a vengeful outsider shortly after, unattractive bore with eccentric clothing at thirteen, followed by the pompous vicar at fourteen. Shylock was the part I had enjoyed most. I played it like Sweeney Todd, brandishing my mother's borrowed carving knife and wearing a yellow cap and a black preaching gown borrowed off my father. My hair was long at the time and I pulled it round to form a long mousy beard.

While my parts had become more respectable with the years they were certainly not the glamour roles I craved. Titania gave me that chance. One of the boys took some indecent-looking photos of me getting a leg over Bottom that sold at a premium to the pupils of Ealing Grammar. I only wish I had bought a copy myself.

I believed in my own sex appeal, but I was intrinsically what the French would call *jolie laide*. Men certainly noticed me when I walked into a room, but they often did nothing afterwards. I looked sexy but I wasn't a status symbol girlfriend. My teeth and features were slightly irregular. My clothes were colourful and strange homemade creations. Often I was so ahead of fashion by some inner instinct that I just got thought odd. My skirts would rise or fall even before Vogue had thought of a new length and I would experiment with huge homemade jewellery, or pearls in my hair. I was someone men wanted to shag but not to be seen out with. It was only when I went to Art School that I was to encounter any people like myself.

Chapter Twenty-Five: The Power of Greek

WE WERE GIVEN a common room in the Sixth. At the end of my first term I brought home my coffee mug. "Can I have another?" I asked. "This one's got dirty!" My mother was horrified to see it had green mould on it. I explained that most of the girls' mugs were in the same state. The cloakrooms or labs with access to running water were at the other end of the school. Tea bags and last half-inches of coffee were thrown out of the windows. We usually remembered to look for passers-by first. Nothing got a wash until the end of term.

Some people used the common room for smoking until that was put a stop to. Mostly we read trashy magazines there, or played cards. I became friends with a new girl, Lalita. She was Indonesian. Her father was Muslim and her mother a Christian. I found her world fascinating in that she was equally happy with either Allah or the Christian God and could go from Mosque to Church quite happily. She was also rather good at fortune telling and taught me how to do it with cards. Out of school uniform she could look glamorous and seemed to have more interesting dates than the rest of us put together. The secret of her success was the fact that her parents destined her for an arranged marriage. This did not appear to be the horror we might have thought it would be. Three possible candidates had been lined up for her. One was Jewish, which meant that she had to feel able to take yet another religion on board. The three men were all rich, reasonably good-looking and a few years older than her. Altogether her social life seemed very much to be envied. I rather wished that my parents had been able to line up three rich suitors for me.

Mrs. Thomas, our Art teacher, had suggested that those of us who were taking the A-level should go and do some proper life drawing in evening classes. Mum was enthusiastic, as she had enjoyed drawing as a hobby while she was in the Civil Service. I had coloured in some of her nudes as a child.

On Mondays and Wednesdays I cycled to classes in West Ealing. As the evenings grew darker I took the bus. On Mondays we were taught by a couple called the Proctors and on Wednesdays by Mr. Smith. All our teachers seemed to be elderly. Mr. Smith had wonderful patience with the pensioners who had no talent. I was mostly allowed to get on with it more or less. The Proctors on Monday were slightly more impatient with the models who were a mildly eccentric bunch. Mr. Smith used to suffer endless wind-ups from a Polish one who longed to do shoulder-stands by the windows in the full view of passers-by. She also always refused to remove her amber necklace. She was plump and one of the other models was positively fat. The fattest one had a penchant for sitting in an old-fashioned wooden armchair with a curved back. Her flesh would slip out between the ornamental slats of the chair. Occasionally she couldn't resist talking as she modelled. She belonged to the "Uglies" agency and was also a film extra and bit part actress. I've occasionally seen her in small roles in commercials. She still seems to be going strong. She had rather a small squeaky voice, which used to tickle the younger members of the class. After about the first twenty minutes she couldn't resist piping up with something like: "I took my kitty to the vet, today!" She talked a lot about her kitty. I suppose it was marginally less funny than saying "pussy".

The male models always seemed to wear jock straps, which seemed a bit of a cheat. When I went to Art School later, everyone was genuinely naked. One of our male models had false teeth, a complete set, and he'd clash and grind with these from time to time. The rest were younger, more attractive men.

On Saturday mornings I went to another drawing class. All the students were young and the models were clothed. The man with the grinding teeth turned up, and inevitably, he had a dirty Mac. Most of the women models were extremely pretty though. Yet I never got all that much pleasure from that class. I had no urge to draw clothes on bodies. I liked to see straight to the flesh.

Lawrence from Ealing Grammar also attended the Saturday class. His attitude was different to mine. He always seemed slightly embarrassed by nudity when he encountered it later at Art School. There was a touch of prudishness about him. He was not exactly religious, but his mother had been a Catholic and some of that had entered his education. I find that few British Catholics are completely comfortable with nudity.

At school, I was studying four A-level subjects. I had two teachers for Latin, three for Greek, one each for Art and Religious Knowledge. Mrs. Werenick whose daughter Jane was studying Art with me, was one of the nicest teachers in Haberdashers'. I remember the utter patience with which she stood my wind-ups. I engaged her in endless theological discussions. My co-pupils were delighted in that it meant they could read or write letters through entire class sessions. I have never been able to resist a dialectical argument. I even once applied many of Isaiah's prophecies to Judas rather than Jesus. Mrs. Werenick was never able to refute my arguments. Indeed, once I thought about it, a lot of those suffering prophecies could apply as much to the one as to the other.

Pompey and Phoebe still showed some vague disapproval where I was concerned. A trip to a symposium was arranged and we were all auditioned. One of us was to be chosen to recite a Horace poem: "O fons Bandusiae" which is addressed to a spring. To Pompey's horror, I was the only one who could scan it well enough to read it in the right rhythm. I read it perfectly first time, while their favourites stumbled through. There was a strange reason behind my facility with this particular ode. My mother had sung it to me constantly as a lullaby. Somehow my subconscious memory from that time made me recite the words correctly. One of my fans might see another explanation. A few years ago, someone wrote to tell me that I am a reincarnation of the poet Horace. While I have always liked his poetry and found it easier to translate than my co-pupils, I have some doubts...Why, oh why, don't I remember more Latin?

I was still enjoying Greek. Mrs. Z as we called her, lived next door to Hannah. Both their gardens ran down to the Thames. Mrs. Z had a regular boat-race party every year. We were all invited. Hannah changed course soon and came to join our class. She had a good all-round brain, so she was able to swap from studying sciences to Classics with a little extra tuition from her neighbour.

I still think with horror about the make-up that I wore to poor Mrs. Z's party. Barbara Levy and I had volunteered to help make sandwiches or put food on plates beforehand. I applied my make-up by dim light in the early morning. I had plucked my eyebrows almost completely out and covered the whole eye area with pink and purple shadow. It didn't look too bad in the dimness of my bedroom, but the whole horror was revealed in the bright daylight of a lunchtime party in the open air. From a distance I looked like a panda, close-up it was more like a battered teenage bride.

When I was more discreet with make-up I could get away with a little at school. The palest green eye gloss or a smidgen of mascara hardly showed. Once away from school en route for my acting at Ealing Grammar, or an art class, I could shed the school blouse and wear a tight jumper. The school's discreet grey skirt combined reasonably well with other things like tight angora jumpers. At weekends my clothes were far more outrageous. From my earliest teens I had gone through all phases of mini and maxi skirts. I had also bought a chrome yellow, almost fluorescent yachting Mac. It was extremely durable. I only recently passed it on. I sometimes wore it over a purple dress Mum had worn in the last War. I winched my waist in cruelly with a tight belt and curled the hair round my face in tendrils for a slightly Edwardian effect. It was at about this stage that I discovered charity shops and jumble sales and my wardrobe grew and grew. I sometimes worked the odd afternoon in a GLAD charity shop in the holidays. Jumble sale clothes were much better value though. The going rate seemed to be a penny. I favoured items from the Thirties to Fifties. I got my mother in on jumble sales too. Though most of my purchases from those days have dropped to pieces, I still have one cherry silk cocktail dress that is still going strong. I think that was one of my mother's finds.

While I was still enjoying my A-level subjects, by the end of my first year in the Sixth I was going more and more towards Art in my life. Girls who were supposed to be going to Oxford or Cambridge also had an extra class to coach us. We were given a reading list of politically correct literature to tell us what to think and what to discuss at the interview. I have managed to avoid most of that book list to the present day. We were also told which newspapers we should read. Something about the whole situation was beginning to jar. I managed to avoid reading both the book list and the correct newspapers and bluffed my way through any essays that were set. When asked to write about pollution, for instance, not having read the right newspapers I decided to twist my subject and go for the pollution of the English language. I maintained that it had been watered down and generally spoiled since the days of Mediaeval Poetry. I did know something about the latter, even if I knew bugger all about current affairs.

I think the "Oxbridge Class" was one of the causes for my subsequent revolt against the system. It initiated in me a kind of queasiness of the soul. I knew from my Latin classes that education meant leading out. Yet, what was being sold to me in Haberdashers' was closing in and closing ranks, not leading out. Both the book list and the idea of correct newspapers were the product of intellectual snobbery. The book list contained no works of great artistic merit,

no classics even. It was simply a list of non-fiction works that would
prime us in topics to discuss, from current affairs to literary and
artistic criticism. Thus primed we could avoid the danger of thinking for ourselves and expressing our own opinions.

We had been allowed a modicum of choice in which set books
we took for A-level in Latin and Greek. But we only had liberty to
choose between two or three titles in each genre. For Latin we had
Livy and Virgil. For Greek it was Plato and Euripides. Much to
Pompey's dissatisfaction there was mass rebellion against
Thucydides. A year or two ago, in Greece, I told some Greeks that
I had always found him the hardest author when I studied at school.
"We can't understand him either!' they admitted. Instead of
Thucydides we were allotted one of Plato's least likeable dialogues.
Why did examiners set "Laches" when there were so many more
interesting books in Plato's Works? At the time I liked best the dia-
logues surrounding Socrates' death. And they are certainly beauti-
ful pieces of writing. Many years after school I came on the
Phaedrus, a thoroughly Pagan discussion on the nature of love.
How much more fun than Laches that would have been. Yet schools
rarely choose that beautiful dialogue, perhaps because there's an
aura of homosexual flirtation between Socrates and his pupil.
Perhaps also it's considered unacceptable because it shows clearly
that Socrates was a polytheist and not the pre-Christian monothe-
ist that Victorian writers tried to sell us as a role model.

Studying Phaedrus might have made us think for ourselves and
that would have been dangerous. Even to this day there is more
power in the Classics than most people realise. Assuming my son
has no radical objections I would like to teach him Latin and Greek
as soon as he is a competent reader. That way he would go on to
become far more competent at those languages than his mother and
would have a real education to draw on, however little conventional schooling offers him.

In the summer I suffered a kind of semi-mystical anti-conversion on the A21. My faith in both the Haberdashers' system and the
path that I was following melted away. I had gone on one of my long
cycles – London to Hastings by out-of-date maps that didn't show
the newest roads. The detours I had to make because of this and losing my way added about fifteen miles to my route. It was a fiendish-
ly hot day and eighty miles without a hat and without drinking any
water brought on a bout of sunstroke. As I cycled, and later as I was

ill, one line of Euripides' Medea, my other Greek set book, ran through my head. I can still remember it to this day. Medea speaks the words to Apollo: "*Phlox ouraniou dia mou kephalou baine!*" (Flame of heaven pierce through my head.)

The Sun God did in fact strike me down, although on that first day I felt nothing but saddle sore. Within a few days I was feverish and sick and during that time I knew somehow that my path in life had to change irrevocably. I was now a hundred per cent sure that Art mattered more than the pathetic petty concerns of a school. I knew I had to make some kind of a stand about that. Such was the power of one line of Greek poetry...

Chapter Twenty-Six: A Winter's Tale

AT LAST, IN THE second year of the Sixth, we were allowed to wear
our own clothes. They had to be discreet though, which was not
always easy. I brought out my Bonnie and Clyde suit from years
before. The purple maxi skirt teamed with various jumpers might
well fit the bill. Hair still had to be tied back away from the face. I
took to having mine in a ponytail held by a purple suede lace or
beads on elastic.

For the last few months my health hadn't been good, especially
in the period leading up to my lightning anti-conversion. I was suffering several migraines a week and fainting pretty frequently. It was
all, I'm quite sure, just the effects of stress. While I was continuing
in a path that was wrong for me the ill health continued. Once I
changed it began to mend. I am quite sure that at least ninety per
cent of the illness in other people springs from a similar cause. Too
many people force themselves into professions that seem correct
rather than choosing jobs they actually like.

My school was horrified when I announced my intention of
going to Art School rather than Cambridge. They couldn't have
slated my intended profession more if I'd been applying for a job in
a brothel. Everything teachers said tended to the opinion that Art
was not an academic subject and therefore not a viable option for
anyone of intelligence. I thought back to the great Renaissance
artists and their wisdom and I knew that my teachers were completely and utterly wrong.

In the next few weeks everyone tried to dissuade me, but I stuck
to my guns and indeed went further. Mrs. Thomas, the Art teacher,
didn't have immense faith in my artistic abilities and told me I'd
have to work terribly hard if I was to get into a good art school. The
entry rate for the one I most wanted, Chelsea, was about one out of
every forty applicants, according to her. In other words, it was far
harder to get in there than Oxford or Cambridge. It was probably a
subtle and less nasty way of backing the other teachers, but I was
able to use it against them. If entry to Art School was so selective,
then I would need to work all out on that, I said, thus countering
the former argument of teachers that I should give up the non-aca-
demic A-level to concentrate on my three other "proper" subjects.
I already had enough O-levels to meet entry requirements, so I told
my school I would do no A-levels at all. There was no point. I put

in my notice. I would do Art alone till the end of term and then quit to study alone.

As I had no objection to Latin and Greek, I finished my set books before I turned them in. I even copied the whole of Medea out by hand in beautiful writing. While my English handwriting is much like that on doctor's prescriptions, my Greek is totally legible like a scribe's.

Phoebe and Pompey were probably quite glad to lose me. They'd known there was something wrong with me all along. I was sorrier to lose Mrs. Z's lessons. I liked her eccentric enthusiastic approach. Yet, leaving subjects I loved was all part of what I had to do at that moment in time. I still have no regrets for that, just as I have no regrets for retaining my Welsh accent. In both cases, I was making a stand against an intolerable and wrong attitude in the people around me.

From time to time I still meet others who endorse the Haberdashers' position – journalists or writers who assume I must be stupid because I didn't go through the Oxbridge system. Only recently, John Walsh, a literary editor who was the product of that particular branch of education found out I had not read a particular Amis novel. "Ah, the things I could have taught you if we'd been an item!" he exclaimed.

My interview for Chelsea was to be in the spring. I would have to get together a large portfolio. After her initial doubts, Mrs Thomas was helpful and encouraging, getting me to mount everything on coloured paper or card. I worked in the Art Room every day and continued my evening classes. Soon there were several hundred drawings and paintings in my portfolio.

Portfolios are difficult things to manage. Fortunately my arms had grown exceedingly long because my parents had kept ruder books on higher shelves. Even so, as a teenager, it was a strain to fit my arm round a bulging portfolio. One day, as I was carrying it, my hair started to come out of the elastic that was holding it back. In this slightly disreputable state I encountered Miss Dodson whose temper was almost the equal of Miss Ashley's. She ordered me to tie up my hair at once. The corridor was crowded with girls filing in opposite directions. I explained perfectly politely that I would do so as soon as I reached the cloakroom and was able to put down the portfolio. That was not good enough and I was ordered to do it at once. I thought for a moment about dropping the portfolio on her foot but then took the kinder option of insisting that it was only practicable to do it in the cloakroom once I'd offloaded what I was carrying. I said this then moved away. From halfway down the corridor Miss Dodson barked out her orders and I shouted my reiterated objections. At least a hundred girls drank it all in and went on to their lessons happy. No one had defied that particular teacher for years.

What Miss Dodson hated was the whole image I presented – the artist with a file of drawings, the young girl with perky tits, a thin waist and shiny clean hair slipping out of the band that restrained it. I've occasionally seen this irrational hatred from the old to the young, from those without much future to those with one. I remember, years later, a tiny pretty Jamaican girl chattering away on a bus. Her mother and grandmother were with her. An old Polish woman proceeded to attack the child with a venomous torrent of racial abuse. I swapped places with the child to try and get her out of firing range, and joined her mother and grandmother in shouting at the vicious old lady. Somehow, I didn't feel the situation was principally about racism. If it had been, surely she would have attacked the mother and grandmother as well? When the family got off, I also got off at the same stop and said that I believed the old girl was simply jealous. She had no future and she saw a girl before her who was pretty and who sounded clever and happy, judging by the way she talked. She seized on any grounds she could think of to attack. And so it was with Miss Dodson. If I had been thoroughly unattractive and carried no portfolio, I feel sure she would not have come down quite so hard on the little matter of a ponytail coming undone.

As I was leaving at the end of term I was able to go in another play with Ealing Grammar School. If A-levels had been looming on the horizon this would have been banned. The play was *A Winter's Tale* and I won the role of Paulina. It's one of Shakespeare's longest parts and seems to require a lot of fast-speaking simply to get through it all on time. I taught myself to speak faster, a talent which occasionally comes in useful these days when I want to vary the speed in reading aloud a section of a poem, or get an opinion in fast on a radio or TV chat show.

Lawrence and Stephen had a hand in the costume design. The court scenes were Byzantine. I wore a long cream dress covered by a kind of brown cope with a gold criss-cross pattern painted on to the fabric. I plaited my hair into earphones, weaving gold tinsel ribbon into it and pinning it in place with hairgrips with pearls stitched on to them. I rather liked the hairdo I'd evolved and sometimes wore it with modern clothes. Halfway through the play I changed into shepherdess gear and let my hair down. I was doubling as another part for these scenes.

Ralph who had played Bottom the previous year was to be Leontes. The English master had total faith in his abilities, but the rest of us began to wonder when he hadn't learned his lines and was still reading from the book at the dress rehearsal. The first night came and Leontes, we were told, was having a breakdown. Some of us speculated unkindly on those unlearnt lines. The English master had to step in to read the part with book and torch. He had a beautiful voice, poetic as Henry Irving, so we all assumed things would be all right. Sadly, he hadn't practised speed-reading. On that night and the following ones, Shakespeare's "two-hour traffic of the stage" was turned into five hours. Only by the last night had he got it down to a mere four and a half.

There was still a certain amount of horseplay behind the scenes. While my role was more comfortable this time, the main target appeared to be a religious boy who was playing the messenger. His Ribena was laced with garlic, causing him to vomit. Then, someone tampered with the lighting so that the audience saw through his robe down to the Y-fronts as he ascended the steps of the stage.

The girls in the other parts were all culled from other schools. Most of us had flirtations with various boys. Max Lesser who was playing the small part of my husband got ideas about me. He was tall and good-looking enough certainly. I went out with him a couple of times. On the surface he would have seemed ideal for a relationship. My mother certainly thought so. Yet, he reminded me of the Haberdashers' point of view. Most of his beliefs were conventional and he was short on humour. The latter fact meant that I could not resist giving him a cup of tea from a pot I had made at school. It was in the shape of a monster, foursquare, four-legged, bug-eyed and prickle-backed. I enjoyed the look of horror on his face as the Earl Grey sputtered out between its teeth.

That Christmas I avoided a date with Max in order to join Lawrence helping at a children's party at the Chelsea Arts Club, unaware that many years later I would become a member. I liked Lawrence's company more at the time. I was beginning to think that he might be gay though. My parents had tried to instill a prejudice against homosexuality in me. Yet, as I began to meet real live homosexuals I found I had more in common with minds that had opened themselves up to other possibilities.

My love of Shakespeare and the theatre was to continue. As I made new friends across the years I found that I felt easiest with artists and actors or musicians. many were homosexual but I don't think I could be described as a fag-hag. Their sexuality seemed irrelevant. It was their own business, nothing more. I liked them because they had some worthwhile purpose to their life. Consistently, I've found those particular professions contained the most moral people I know. They were not simply seeking a qualification followed by a steady job, Haberdashers' style. They wished to inform, entertain and educate others – the education of "leading out" not "closing in". Everything else was irrelevant to them. They felt no need to conform on petty matters.

I was interviewed for both Chelsea and Ealing Art Schools. Ealing, being an inferior art school, scoffed at my lack of modernity and told me to go and look at an exhibition in the Hayward. They did however accept me. The Chelsea interview, by contrast, was pleasanter. The amount of solid life drawing I'd done was considered a plus not a minus. And Patrick Simons, who was to teach me later on, liked my botanical drawings, too. I was accepted there and only needed to return to Haberdashers' once, to return the portfolio I had borrowed.

For the next few months, after I left school, I marked time before entering a world where I could find other kindred spirits. Every hour of my day was taken up with art. I went to daytime classes as well and learned sculpture; sometimes I brought work home with me to finish. I was the only person in the classes going on to art school. Essentially everyone else was treating Art as a hobby. Some were pensioners, others were bored housewives. While I enjoyed the classes and learned a lot through the amount of practice they gave me, I was not yet in a world where I was to feel in any way at home. While amateur art can occasionally be pleasing, there's a wide gulf in attitude between the amateur and the professional. Years later when I learned to sing I tried one of Tosca's songs: *Vissi d'arte* – I have lived for Art. Perhaps that defines it. Perhaps the decision to go in for what's on the surface impractical and often poorly paid is what separates us from those who wish to treat art as a hobby or therapy. We in the Arts are the risk-takers, the merchants who've sold all for 'the pearl of great price'.

Books by Fiona Pitt-Kethley

London
Rome
Tower of Glass
Gesta
Sky Ray Lolly
Private Parts
Journeys to the Underworld
The Perfect Man
The Misfortunes of Nigel
The Maiden's Progress
Literary Companion to Sex
Dogs
Too Hot to Handle
The Pan Principle
Literary Companion to Low Life
Cabinet of Curiosities
Double Act
Memo from a Muse

New from The Tamworth Press
Red Light Districts of the World
My Schooling: The Autobiography Part One
Baker's Dozen

Also from the Tamworth Press

Coincidences by James Plaskett